SMP 11-16

Book B+

CAMBRIDGE
UNIVERSITY PRESS

Published by the Press Syndicate of the University of Cambridge
The Pitt Building, Trumpington Street, Cambridge CB2 1RP
40 West 20th Street, New York, NY 10011–4211, USA
10 Stamford Road, Oakleigh, Melbourne 3166, Australia

First published 1994

Produced by Gecko Limited, Bicester, Oxon.

Printed in Great Britain by Scotprint Ltd., Musselburgh

A catalogue record for this book is available from the British Library

ISBN 0 521 45793 9 paperback

Cover photograph of St Basil's Cathedral, Moscow. Tony Stone Images, David Sutherland

Contents

1 Tables, charts and networks

A Borrowing

You may have seen loan repayment tables in newspapers.
These show how much has to be paid back each month.
This depends on how long the loan is taken out for and
how much is borrowed.

A1 Siobhan would like to buy a second-hand car.
She has saved £200 as a deposit but needs to
borrow £1000.

This table shows the amount she will have to repay each
month for different loans and repayment periods.

Amount borrowed (£s)	Period of repayment in months			
	12	24	36	48
500	45·42	24·58	17·64	14·17
750	68·13	36·88	26·46	21·25
1000	90·83	49·17	35·28	28·33
2000	181·67	98·33	70·56	56·67
5000	454·17	245·83	176·39	141·67

> If Siobhan borrows £500 for 48 months then she must repay £14·17 a month.

(a) If Siobhan borrows £1000 over 24 months, how much will
she pay each month?

(b) How much will she pay altogether?

(c) How much would she have to pay each month if she
borrowed £1000 for 48 months?

(d) A friend of Siobhan says:

Is he right?
Back-up your answers
with some figures
and calculations.

> You're far better off taking out a loan for as long as possible! Just look at the repayments in the table. It's a gift!

A2 Ruth also needs to borrow £1000. She can afford to pay £10 *each week*.
For how long will her loan be?

A3 The repayment figures in the table were for 1993.
Find a repayment table in one of this week's newspapers.
How much would Siobhan have to pay a month to borrow £1000
over 24 months now?

B Two-way tables

Tables can be very useful for displaying complicated information.

B1 Sixty-three students are making their
option choices for P. E.
Hockey and badminton are available.
45 wanted to play hockey, 29 did *not*
want to play badminton and 21 wanted
to play both badminton and hockey.

One way of showing this information
clearly is to use a **two-way table**.

Copy and complete this two-way table.
Use it to find how many students wanted to do neither hockey
nor badminton (not hockey and not badminton).
(You will find it useful to compare this table with the choices.
It will help you understand how the two-way table works.)

	Hockey	Not hockey	Total
Badminton	21		
Not badminton			29
Total	45		63

B2 Here is a two-way table showing the results of a car survey
involving makes and colours. Copy and complete the table.

	Ford	Not Ford	Total
Red	20	50	
Not red	60	300	
Total			

(a) How many cars were surveyed?

(b) How many Ford cars were involved in the survey?

(c) How many Ford cars were a colour other than red?

(d) What was the total number of red cars surveyed?

B3 Mrs Chandra asked the 233 pupils in Year 9 where they wanted to
go for the end-of-year outing. The two choices were Alton Towers or
Blackpool. Of these, 148 did not want to go to Blackpool, 91 did not want
to go to Alton Towers and 23 did not want to go to either place.

Complete this two-way table to help you find out how many people were
prepared to go to either venue.

	Alton Towers	Not Alton Towers	Total
Blackpool			
Not Blackpool			
Total			

2

C Mileage charts

Mileage charts are usually found in road atlases.

This mileage chart gives the distances by road between seven towns and cities in the north of England.

> For example, the distance between Leeds and Newcastle is 95 miles.

Hull						
61	Leeds					
131	75	Liverpool				
99	43	35	Manchester			
89	66	141	109	Middlesbrough		
126	95	170	139	41	Newcastle	
94	74	130	72	132	161	Nottingham

C1 How far is it:

(a) from Leeds to Middlesbrough

(b) from Hull to Nottingham

(c) from Newcastle to Liverpool?

C2 Which two towns or cities are nearest to each other?

C3 Calculate the total distance travelled by Siobhan on this journey:

Hull → Manchester → Liverpool → Hull.

C4 Derek works for a publisher. He is based in Liverpool and has to call on bookshops in Leeds, Hull and Manchester.

Which route should he take to keep his mileage as low as possible?

C5 Lisa lives in Hull.

(a) She wants to visit the other six towns, one each day, returning home each evening. Find a simple way of working out her total mileage from the table.

(b) Instead Lisa invites one person from each of the six other towns to a meeting in Hull. What is the total mileage travelled?

(c) In which town should Lisa have the meeting so that the total mileage travelled by all seven people is as small as possible? Explain your method.

C6 This is a map showing some towns in Norfolk and the main roads connecting them. The distance between two towns is shown on the road between them.

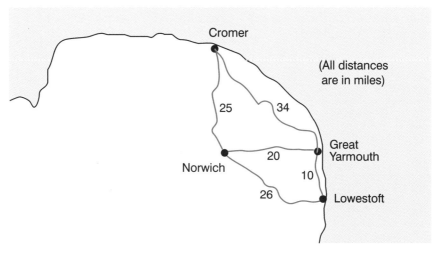

(a) Draw up a mileage chart showing the distances between the towns. If there is a choice of routes use the one with the shortest distance.

(b) If you start and finish at Norwich, what is the shortest total distance you can travel if you visit all the towns?

C7 Here are the distances between some towns and cities in Ireland. Draw up a mileage chart from this information.

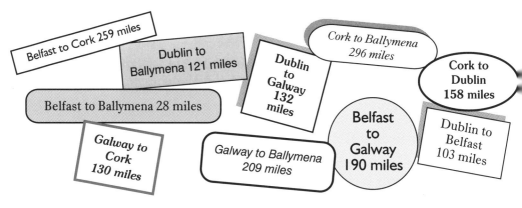

*O*ption

Draw a mileage chart for the five towns or cities nearest to your school. You could use your chart to display approximate travelling times instead of distances. Times are more useful to some people.

Networks

Five people are going on a package holiday together. Amir is already friends with Debbie and Eric, who are friends with each other. Bea is friends with Carl, Debbie and Eric. Carl is also friends with Debbie.

This information can be represented as a network diagram or a link table.

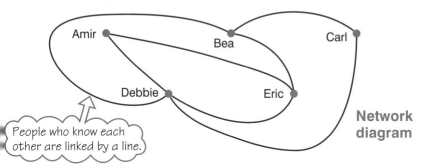

Network diagram

People who know each other are linked by a line.

	Amir	Bea	Carl	Debbie	Eric
Amir	0	0	0	1	1
Bea	0	0	1	1	1
Carl	0	1	0	1	0
Debbie	1	1	1	0	1
Eric	1	1	0	1	0

Link table

If two people know each other there is a '1' in the link table. When two people do not know each other there is a '0' in the link table.

For example, by looking along the top row you can see that Amir knows Debbie and Eric but not Bea or Carl.

D1 Who is friends with everyone?

D2 Who is friends with the least number of people?

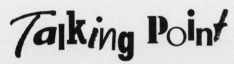

Why does the link table have a line of symmetry?

D3 The families in Acacia Close are sending New Year's cards to each other. The information about who sends cards to whom is given in this network diagram.

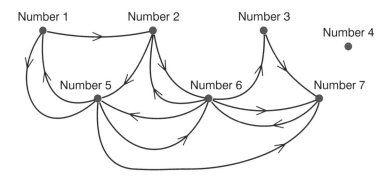

(a) The people in *Number 1* sent a card to *Number 2*.
But they did not get one in return.
How can you tell this from the network diagram?

(b) Which houses received most cards?

(c) Which house sent the most cards?

(d) Which house in the close is probably empty?

Talking Point

How could you draw a link table for the network diagram above?
Does the link table have a line of symmetry?

D4 There are four villages labelled P, Q, R and S on the island of Druc. They are linked by tracks. The link table shows how they are connected.

(a) Draw a network diagram showing how the villages are connected.

(b) Which village is the most cut off?

	P	Q	R	S
P	0	1	1	1
Q	1	0	1	0
R	1	1	0	0
S	1	0	0	0

There are special names which we use with networks. The town, person or whatever is marked with a dot is called a **vertex**. The **order of a vertex** is the number of links it has. The plural of vertex is **vertices**.

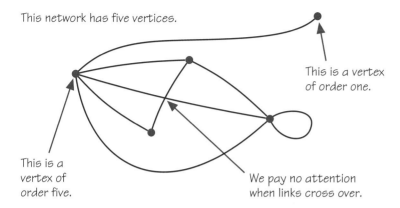

This network has five vertices.

This is a vertex of order one.

This is a vertex of order five.

We pay no attention when links cross over.

This network has 4 odd order vertices and 1 even order vertex.

D5 See how many of these networks you can draw.

(a) A network with three vertices which are all of order two.

(b) A network which has four vertices, two of even order and two of odd order.

(c) A network of four vertices, all of which are of odd order.

D6 Make a list of some tables, charts and networks you have used recently (but not in this chapter).

Puzzle

Make a copy of this diagram. The object of the puzzle is to connect A to *a*, B to *b*, and so on, without any lines crossing (including the ones already on the diagram).

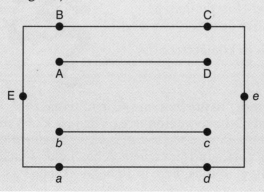

2 Pencil and paper 1

(a chapter for two people)

A Try 'n' check

A1 Investigate these patterns of numbers.
You will need to continue some of them.
Jot down anything interesting you notice.

(a) $10 \times 12 =$
$100 \times 12 =$
$1000 \times 12 =$
$\vdots \qquad \vdots$

(b) $2 \times 13 =$
$20 \times 13 =$
$200 \times 13 =$
$\vdots \qquad \vdots$

(c) $2 \times 6 =$
$20 \times 60 =$
$200 \times 600 =$
$\vdots \qquad \vdots$

(d) $2 \times 2 =$
$20 \times 20 =$
$200 \times 200 =$
$\vdots \qquad \vdots$

A2 Explain with a few sentences or diagrams how to work out
the answers to questions like these **without** using a calculator.

30×12 $\qquad$ 300×7 $\qquad$ 400×23

A3 Here are some calculations and their answers.
Check them without using a calculator.
Write down the correct answer for those that are wrong.

(a) $60 \times 70 = 4200$ (b) $60 \times 60 = 360$

(c) $600 \times 5 = 300$ (d) $15 \times 30 = 450$

(e) $800 \times 20 = 1600$ (f) $900 \times 2 = 1800$

(g) $800 \times 12 = 9600$ (h) $7 \times 300 = 2100$

A4 Idris is a keen 400 m runner.
In training, he runs 12 practice
races a week. How far does he
run in practice distances in a week?

What is this in kilometres?

A5 In a roll of toilet tissue there are 40 m of tissue.
What length of tissue would there be in a pack of 6 rolls?

A6 Packet soup comes in 16 g sachets. A box holds 4 sachets.
What weight of soup is there in 10 boxes of soup?

Most of the mistakes we make when using a calculator probably involve pressing the correct keys – but in the wrong order.
For example, you might key in 74 × 22, instead of 47 × 22.

You can usually find errors where digits have been entered in the wrong order by working out roughly what the answer should be.

The secret is to look at the calculation and to round the numbers to give a rough calculation which **you** can do in **your** head. Here are two examples.

47 is about 50 and 22 is quite near to 20. So 50 × 20 = 1000 seems reasonable.

47 × 22

47 is close to 45 and 22 is about 20. So a rough answer is 45 × 20 = 900.

A7 (a) Use your calculator to work out 47 × 22.

(b) Who was closer, Frank or Becky?

A8 (a) Estimate the answers to these calculations.

(i) 31 × 39   (ii) 48 × 21   (iii) 52 × 8   (iv) 18 × 19

(b) Use your estimates to match each calculation with the correct calculator display.

A | 342

B | 416

C | 1209

D | 1008

(c) Check your answers with a calculator

A9 With additions, the order of adding does not matter.
For example, 5 + 9 has the same value as 9 + 5.

Does the order matter with:

(a) multiplication   (b) division   (c) subtraction?

Experiment for yourselves.

Do not use a calculator to do questions A10 to A13.

A10 Isha is a keen jogger. She runs a 13 km circuit three times a week. About how many kilometres would this be in a year? (There are 52 weeks in a year.)

A11 Selma goes to school 38 weeks a year. She walks 22 km to and from school each week. About how far is this in a year?

A12 Ira buys two magazines a week. They cost £1·49 and £1·75 each. About how much does she spend on magazines each year?

A13 It is charities week at Central High School. The number of pupils is 713. If each pupil were to collect £6·75, roughly what would the total collected be?

Estimation game

This is a game for two. You will need four 0–9 dice.

- Throw the four dice and write down the numbers showing.
    5   7   3   5

- Arrange these four numbers into a 4-digit number in any way you wish. This is your target number.
  For example: 3755

- Each player has to make a multiplication from the four digits whose answer is as close as possible to their target number.
  For example: 75 × 53 = 3975 – not too bad!
              Is 553 × 7 closer?
  Allow about two minutes for this. Afterwards work out each other's multiplications with a calculator.

- Scoring is as follows:
    within 100 of the target .... 5 points
    within 200 .... 3 points
    within 500 .... 2 points
    within 1000 .... 1 point

- Play the game until one of you reaches ten points.

Make up a dice game for yourselves which involves estimating.
Try the game out on some people in your group.

B Pick 'n' mix

On the next few pages are some pencil-and-paper methods for working out the calculation 532 × 14.
You will need to look at each of them together.

B1 This method has been used all over the world for several thousand years.

  (a) Imagine having to find 532 × 99, using this method!
Can you think of any short cuts?

```
 532
 532
 532
 532
 532
 532
 532
 532
 532
 532
 532
 532
 532
 532
7448
  4 2
```

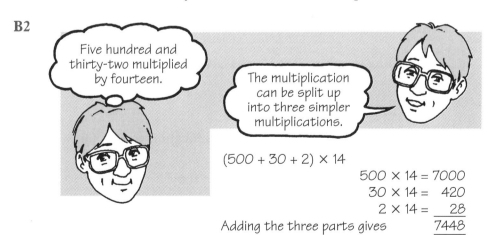

  (b) Find 293 × 7 using this method.

  (c) Emile has this method for checking a multiplication.
He multiplies the last digit of each number.
If the result is the same as the last digit of the answer, then it must be correct.

```
  532
× 14
7448
```

Is Emile correct?
Check this out for yourselves with some multiplications.

B2

Five hundred and thirty-two multiplied by fourteen.

The multiplication can be split up into three simpler multiplications.

$(500 + 30 + 2) \times 14$

$$500 \times 14 = 7000$$
$$30 \times 14 = 420$$
$$2 \times 14 = 28$$

Adding the three parts gives   7448

Use this method to calculate 744 × 16.

B3 Investigate what happens when 2-digit numbers are multiplied by 101. Try to find a similar result for 3-digit numbers.

B4 The answer to the multiplication 14 × 532 is the area of a rectangle measuring 14 by 532 (ignoring units).

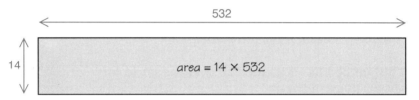

The rectangle can be split up into smaller rectangles like this:

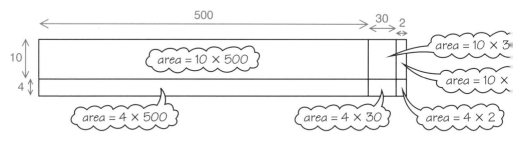

It is usually easier to draw up a multiplication grid …

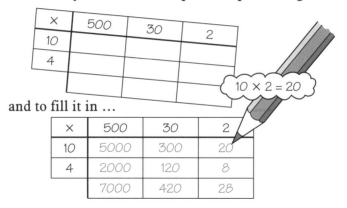

and to fill it in …

×	500	30	2
10	5000	300	20
4	2000	120	8
	7000	420	28

Adding together all the 'areas' gives:
$$5000 + 300 + 20$$
$$+ 2000 + 120 + 8 = 7448$$
so 14 × 532 = 7448.

(a) Copy and complete this multiplication grid for 26 × 162.
What is 26 × 162?

×	100	60	2
20	2000	1200	
6	600		
	2600		

(b) Javed is exactly 15 years old. How many days has he lived?
(Take a year to be 365 days.)

B5 This method is very old and originally came from India. It is sometimes called the window method because the grids look a little like windows.

1 Draw the 'window' grid and write the numbers to be multiplied along the window.

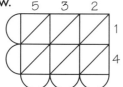

2 Multiply the digits as if you were filling in a multiplication grid.

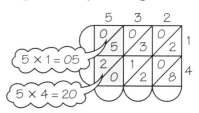

5 × 1 = 05
5 × 4 = 20

3 When all the multiplications are finished add up the numbers along the diagonals, starting from the bottom right of the grid.

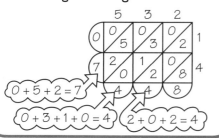

0 + 5 + 2 = 7
0 + 3 + 1 + 0 = 4   2 + 0 + 2 = 4

4 Read the answer from round the outside of the grid.
So 532 × 14 = 7448.

(a) In a book there are 31 lines on a page. How many lines will there be in a book 122 pages long? Use the window method.

(b) Ian is using the window method to find 413 × 72. When he adds along this diagonal he gets an answer of seventeen.

What should he do?
Should he carry over?
Experiment for yourselves.
Check your answer with
a calculator.

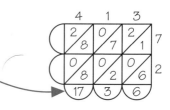

B6 Here is another way of calculating 532 × 14 (or 14 × 532).

Use this method to find the answers to these.

532 × 4 = 2128
532 × 10 = 5320
532 × 14 = 7448

(a) A single paving stone has a mass of 51 kg. What is the mass of 23 of these stones?

(b) One of the largest radishes ever grown weighed 17 pounds. There are 16 ounces in a pound. How many ounces did it weigh?

13

B7 This is an Ancient Egyptian method of multiplication.
All you need do is to double.

$$1 \times 532 = 532 \qquad \text{one lot of 532}$$
$$2 \times 532 = 1064 \qquad \text{two lots of 532}$$
$$4 \times 532 = 2128 \qquad \text{four lots of 532}$$
$$8 \times 532 = 4256 \qquad \text{eight lots of 532}$$

The problem is to find fourteen lots of 532 (14×532).
Fourteen lots of 532 is the same as $(2 + 4 + 8)$ lots of 532.
So $14 \times 532 = 1064 + 2128 + 4256 = 7448$.

(a) Use some of the figures above to find 11×532.

(b) Some kinds of bamboo can grow 91 cm each day!
By how much could this type of bamboo grow in 14 days?

Talking Points

Look back at the six different methods of doing long multiplication.
Are any of them similar?

Do you know any other pencil-and-paper methods for multiplication?

Use whichever pencil-and-paper method or methods you want to answer these.

B8 (a) 321×12 (b) 401×15 (c) 16×311 (d) 412×13

B9 A hundredweight is an old unit of weight. It is 112 pounds.
A prize dairy cow weighs 14 hundredweight. How many pounds is this?

B10 Some diabetics have to have insulin injections. A woman in
New Zealand has had to have one injection of insulin a day
for 49 years. How many injections is this?

B11 In 1980 the world record for the pole vault
was 19 feet.
There are 12 inches in a foot.
1 inch is roughly 25 millimetres.

(a) How many inches was this?

(b) How many millimetres was it?

B12 Zara can write an average of 17 words on a line.
She wrote an essay which was 132 lines long.
About how many words were in the essay?

3 Polygons

A A review

Any shape with straight sides is called a polygon.
The word 'polygon' comes from Greek words meaning 'many corners'.

Some polygons have special names, for example:

5-sided – **pentagon**

6-sided – **hexagon**

7-sided – **heptagon**

8-sided – **octagons**

A1 What is the common name for a 3-sided polygon?

A2 Three people are arguing about the common name for a 4-sided polygon.

What is the common name for a 4-sided polygon?

A3 Draw a 4 by 4 grid of dots.
The example shows a 5-sided polygon or pentagon which has been drawn by joining up dots.

Can you draw a polygon with 6 sides?

What is the largest number of sides a polygon on this grid can have?

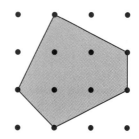

B Exterior angles

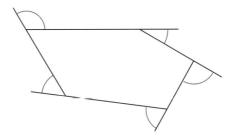

This diagram shows the **exterior** angles of a pentagon.

The exterior angles are **outside** the pentagon.

You need worksheet B + 1 for questions B1 and B2.

B1 (a) Follow these instructions to draw the exterior angles of the pentagon.

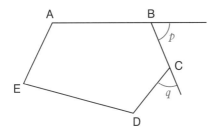

- Extend the line AB by about 5 cm.
  Label the exterior angle p.

- Now extend the line BC.
  Label the exterior angle q.

- Draw the other three exterior angles by extending CD, DE and EA.
  Label these exterior angles r, s and t.

(b) Measure all these exterior angles.

(c) Add together the exterior angles of the pentagon $(p + q + r + s + t)$.

B2 (a) Draw the exterior angles of the hexagon.

(b) Measure the exterior angles.

(c) What is the sum of the exterior angles of the hexagon?

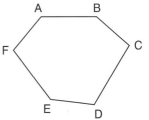

B3 Draw your own pentagon and hexagon.
Find the sum of the exterior angles of your pentagon and the sum of the exterior angles of your hexagon.

Compare your answers to other people's.
What do you notice?

Talking Point

Sometimes it is easy to be confused about which angles are the exterior ones.

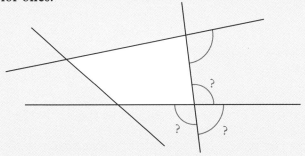

Can you think of any easy way to check?

B4 Draw any quadrilateral. Construct the exterior angles.

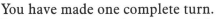

Imagine walking from A to B.

When you reach B you turn through angle p.

Then walk to C and turn through angle q.

Then to D and turn through r.

Then to A and turn through s. You are now facing B.

You have made one complete turn. In other words you have turned through 360°.

So $p + q + r + s = 360°$ (exterior angles sum to 360°).

Check that they add up to 360° by measuring them.

B5 Draw any triangle. Construct the exterior angles. Show that the sum of these angles is 360° by using a similar reasoning to **B4**.

B6 How could you convince someone that the sum of the exterior angles is 360° for an octagon, or any other polygon?

c Regular polygons

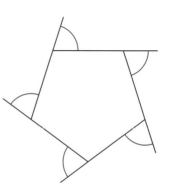

A **regular polygon** has all its sides equal and all its exterior angles equal.

The sum of the exterior angles of this regular pentagon is 360°.

There are five exterior angles.

These are all equal, so each exterior angle is 360° ÷ 5 = 72°.

> **C1** Work out the size of an exterior angle of a regular hexagon.

> **C2** What is the size of an exterior angle of a regular octagon?

The **interior angles** of a polygon are the **inside angles**.

When you know the exterior angle of a regular polygon, you can work out the interior angle. (Remember angles on a straight line sum to 180°.)

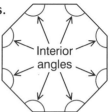

Each exterior angle of this regular pentagon is 72° (360 ÷ 5).

But the exterior angle and the interior angle at A make 180°. (They form a straight line.)

So $z + 72° = 180°$
$z = 108°$

The interior angle of a pentagon is 108°.

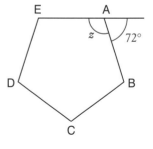

> **C3** Calculate the interior angle of a regular hexagon.

Challenge

Write a LOGO procedure or procedures which will show the exterior angles of regular polygons.
For example:

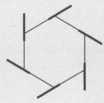

C4 Copy and complete this table. It shows the interior and exterior angles of some regular polygons.

You have already calculated some of the angles.
The others will have to be calculated.

Number of sides	Name	Exterior angle	Interior angle
3			
4			
5			
6			
8			
9	nonagon		
10	decagon		
12	dodecagon		

Two students want to use LOGO to draw some regular polygons.
One of them has written this procedure called TURN:

```
TO TURN " ANGLE
RIGHT :ANGLE
FORWARD 20
END
```

(a) What does this procedure draw if 'ANGLE' is made equal to 90?
Check your answer using LOGO.

(b) One of the students keyed in:
REPEAT 4[TURN 90]
Which regular polygon will it draw? Check using LOGO.

(c) The other student edited the last piece of coding to:
REPEAT 3[TURN 60]
She said it would draw a regular triangle (equilateral triangle).
Was she right? If she was wrong what mistake had she made?

(d) Check your answers to C4 by using LOGO.
You may find the procedures above useful.

D Irregular polygons

A regular polygon is one which has **all sides and angles equal**.
Polygons are *not* always regular!

D1 Sometimes you need to know the sum of the interior angles
of a non-regular polygon. Draw some non-regular
(**irregular**) polygons. Find the sum of their interior angles.

Make a note of anything interesting you find.
You may find it easier to work with a partner.
This will certainly give you more results.

You will have to look at your results carefully, because it is
almost impossible to measure angles exactly.
In fact, measuring to the nearest degree is acceptable.
Here are some results to start you off.

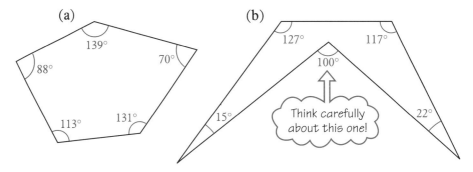

(a)

139°
88°
70°
113° 131°

(b)

127° 117°
100°
15°
Think carefully
about this one!
22°

D2 A diagonal is a straight line drawn from one corner of a polygon
to another. All these blue lines are diagonals.

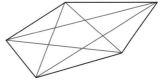

Investigate one or more of these statements.

(a) A pentagon always has five diagonals.

(b) There are as many diagonals as the number of sides of the polygon.

(c) The diagonals of a pentagon form a star.

(d) The diagonals of a pentagon form another pentagon in the centre.

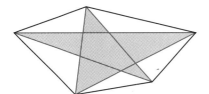
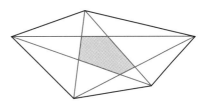

In **D1** you probably found that the sum of the interior angles of a quadrilateral was about 360°, a pentagon about 540°, a hexagon 720°, and so on.

But you can never be sure that your answers are always true. There is nothing to say that there *might* be a case where they are not 360°, 540°, and so on.

We have already convinced ourselves that the sum of the exterior angles of a pentagon is 360°.

From this result we can prove that the sum of the interior angles of a pentagon is always 540°.

The interior and exterior angles at each corner (or vertex) add up to 180°. This is because the sum of the angles on a straight line is 180°.

In this pentagon there are five pairs of exterior and interior angles.
These five pairs of angles add up to 5 × 180°.

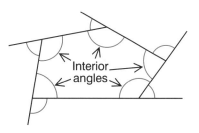

In other words
    5(interior angles) + 5(exterior angles) = 5 × 180°

But we already know that the exterior angles add up to 360°.
So
    5(interior angles) + 360° = 5 × 180°
                              = 900°
From this we can say that
    5(interior angles) = 900° – 360°
                       = 540°

> **The sum of the 5 interior angles of a pentagon is 540°.**

There was nothing special about the pentagon, so it must be true for all pentagons.

D3   This is a hexagon.

(a) What do the 6 exterior and 6 interior angles add up to?

(b) What is the sum of the exterior angles?

(c) What is the sum of the interior angles?

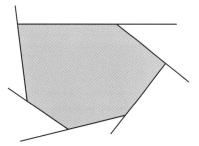

D4 The interior angles of a
pentagon add up to 540°.

Work out the size of angle *a*.

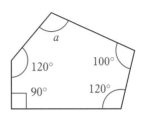

D5 Work out the size of angle *b*
in this diagram.
You may find it useful to
look back at your answer
to **D3**(c).

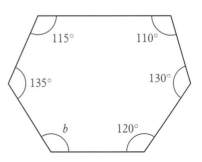

D6 What is the sum of the interior angles of a quadrilateral?

D7 Work out the sum of the interior angles of an octagon.

D8

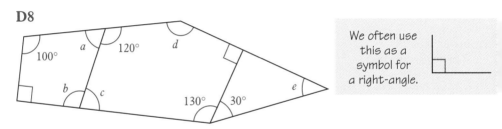

We often use
this as a
symbol for
a right-angle.

Find the values of the lettered angles in this diagram.
Try to explain each step in your working.

D9 The sum of the interior angles of a polygon is 1800°.
How many sides does the polygon have?
(**Hint.** You might find trial and improvement useful.)

D10 Janet has drawn this irregular (non-regular) hexagon.
She says that the sum of its interior angles should be
$4 \times 180° = 720°$ (which is $8 \times 90°$).

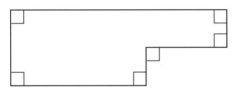

But she totals up the angles in her diagram and says the sum
of the interior angles is $6 \times 90° = 540°$!
What's gone wrong?

E1   This diagram shows three regular polygons that completely
surround the point P. There is no overlap or gap.

(a) What should the angles around P add up to so that
there is no gap or overlap at P?

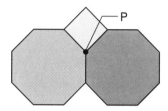

(b) Investigate other arrangements of regular polygons which
completely surround points like P.
If you wish, check your answers by using a polygon stencil.

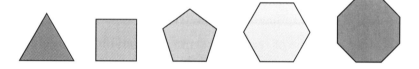

Talking Point

On page 21 it was proved that the sum of the interior angles
of any pentagon is 540°.

Use these diagrams to help you find other proofs that the sum
of the interior angles of a pentagon is 540°.

Try these other methods with some other polygons.

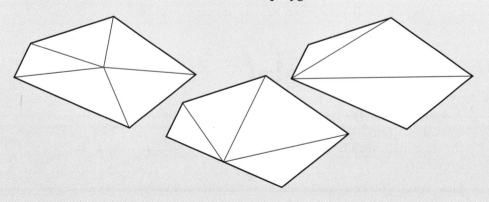

4 Polygons and symmetry

A Reflection symmetry

A1 This regular hexagon has 6 lines
of reflection symmetry.
Hexagons are not always regular.

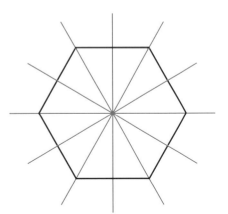

(a) Draw a hexagon with only
2 lines of reflection symmetry.

(b) Draw a hexagon with just 1 line
of reflection symmetry.

(c) Draw a hexagon with exactly
3 lines of reflection symmetry.

A2 Draw some quadrilaterals with:

(a) no lines of reflection symmetry

(b) just one line of reflection symmetry and one right-angle

A3 Draw triangles (if you can) with these numbers of lines of
reflection symmetry:

(a) 0   (b) 1   (c) 2   (d) 3

A4 Is there a connection between the number of equal angles and
the number of lines of reflection symmetry in triangles?
Give examples to support your answer.

A5 Draw pentagons (if you can) with just the following number
of lines of symmetry:

(a) 0   (b) 1   (c) 2   (d) 3   (e) 4   (f) 5

Talking Point

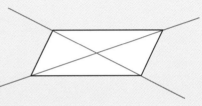

A common mistake is to say that in
a parallelogram like this one,
the diagonals are lines of reflection
symmetry.

How could you convince someone that this is wrong?

Can you name a quadrilateral which has exactly two lines of
reflection symmetry?

B Rotation symmetry

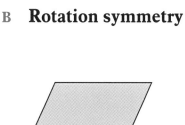 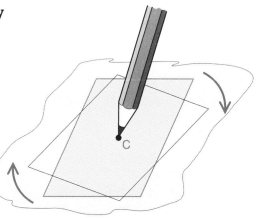

This parallelogram has no lines of symmetry.

But a tracing of it will fit exactly over it twice when rotated about the centre C.

We say that the parallelogram has **rotation symmetry** of order 2.

B1 Complete worksheet B+ 2.

B2 What is the order of rotation symmetry (if they have one) of these polygons? Try to decide without using tracing paper.

(a) 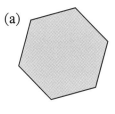 (b) 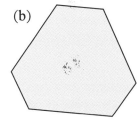 (c)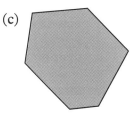

B3 Draw a hexagon which has rotation symmetry of order two. Does your hexagon have any lines of symmetry?

B4 Investigate these two questions.
Draw an example or examples to support your answers.

(a) *Can a shape have rotation symmetry but no reflection symmetry?*

(b) *Can a shape have reflection symmetry without rotation symmetry?*

B5 Draw quadrilaterals (if you can) which only have rotation symmetry of order:

(a) 2   (b) 3   (c) 4

c Line and rotational symmetry

Sometimes reflection symmetry is called **line symmetry** and rotation symmetry is called **rotational symmetry**.

Also, rotation symmetry of order 3 is sometimes called 3-fold rotation symmetry.

C1 This shape has rotational symmetry of order 4.
But it also has line (or reflection) symmetry.

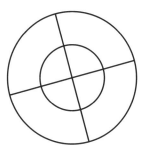

(a) How many lines of symmetry does it have?

(b) What is the angle between each line of symmetry and the next?

(c) If one of the 8 sections of the figure is shaded, the shape has no rotational symmetry and just one line of symmetry.

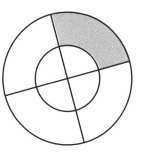

Make a copy of the shape. Shade in another section so that the new shape has two lines of symmetry and rotation symmetry of order two.

C2 Investigate this statement.
In any regular polygon the order of rotation symmetry and number of lines of symmetry is the same number.

C3 Draw polygons which have:

(a) rotation symmetry of order 2 and two lines of symmetry

(b) no rotation symmetry and one line of symmetry

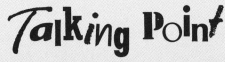

Ela says that all shapes, however irregular, have rotation symmetry of at least order one. Is she correct?

5 Significant figures

A What's significant?

A1 Imagine you were to get this cheque!

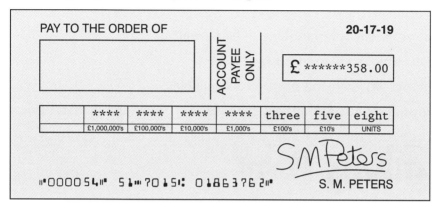

Suppose one of the digits (3, 5 or 8) was one less than it should be.

(a) Which digit would you **not** want this to be?

(b) Which digit would have the least effect on the money you got?

A2 (a) Which is the most important (**significant**) digit in £174?

(b) Which is the least significant digit?

How close?

Do this activity with a partner.

• Jot down a number, for example 463.
This is your target number.

• The aim is to write down another number as close as possible to
this target number. This other number can have as many zeroes as
you need but only one other digit. (You may also use a decimal point.)
Try 400 or 500 or ?

• Experiment with other target numbers such as large numbers,
decimals, and so on.
Can you both agree on a rule to do this activity simply by looking at
the target number? Tell your teacher your rule.

A3 Use your rule on these target numbers.

(a) 287   (b) 43   (c) 43 000   (d) 0·43

In question **A3** you rounded the target numbers to 1 significant figure. (This is sometimes written as 1 s.f.)

So   524 to 1 s.f. is 500, 0·551 to 1 s.f. is 0·6, and so on.

> **A4**   Round each of these numbers to 1 significant figure.
>
>   (a) 5264   (b) 83014   (c) 0·732   (d) 0·916

What to do with 5s when rounding can be a problem.

For example, what is 550 rounded to 1 s.f.?

In fact 550 is exactly half-way between 500 and 600.

We just agree to round up. It makes things easier if we all use the same rule.

Talking Point

| To round to 1 significant figure look at the second most significant figure. If it is 5 or more round up the most significant figure. Otherwise leave it as it is. Finally, write as zero all the figures after the most significant. |

Read this extract with a partner. Does the rule work?
Try it out with some numbers of your own.

Sometimes it is necessary to round to 2 significant figures.
Here are two worked examples.

Round 58 592 to 2 significant figures.	Round 0·41 23 to 2 significant figures.
The two most significant figures are 5 and 8.	The first two significant figures are 4 and 1.
The third significant figure (5) is 5 or more.	The third significant figure (2) is less than 5.
So rounding to 2 s.f. we get 59 000.	So rounding to 2 s.f. we get 0·41.

> **A5**   Round each of these numbers to 2 significant figures.
>
>   (a) 5264   (b) 83 514   (c) 0·775   (d) 0·916
>
> **A6**   Isha is doing the activity 'How close?' She has to get as close to 0·0192 a she can using just two non-zero digits: in other words, to round 0·0192 t 2 significant figures. Eventually she decides on 0·02.
>
>   (a) Was Isha correct? Can you get closer, sticking to the rules?
>
>   (b) Show why 60 909 rounded to 2 significant figures, is *not* 60 900.

28

When we round a number to 2 significant figures we say that the result is **correct** to 2 significant figures.

If there are zeros at the beginning of a number, as in 0·002 76, they do not count as significant figures – the first significant figure is '2'.

But if there are zeros between other digits they count as significant figures. For example, in 4507 the third significant figure is '0' and in 607 the second significant figure is '0'.

Here are some worked examples. Make sure you understand them.

0·000 005 932 correct to 1 s.f. is 0·000 006   606 999 correct to 1 s.f. is 600 000
0·0999 correct to 1 s.f. is 0·1   509 490 correct to 2 s.f. is 510 000

A7 Round each of these numbers to 1 significant figure.

(a) 0·073 21   (b) 0·010 97   (c) 99 000   (d) 0·976 54

(e) 100·953   (f) 103 456   (g) 0·0047   (h) 0·000 010 9

A8 Which digit do you need to look at to round a number to 3 s.f. ?

A9 To how many significant figures do you think these are correct?

(a)   (b)

Daily Bugle
1000 car workers on short time

Daily Exclusive
300 jobs in new building development

(c) News and Views
11 000 shipyard workers laid off

A10 Here is some work on significant figures. Unfortunately there are many mistakes.
Write down the correct answers and explain what is wrong in each one.

(a) 910 correct to 1 s.f. is 9.   (b) 199 correct to 1 s.f. is 100.

(c) 0.094 correct to 2 s.f. is 0.09.   (d) 3499 to 3 s.f. is 350.

A11 The number of people attending an athletics meeting is given in a newspaper as 29 000 correct to 2 significant figures.
What is the smallest and largest the crowd could have been?

A12 To how many significant figures do you think these are given?

(a) The height of Everest is 29 028 feet.

(b) The circumference of the Earth is 40 million metres.

29

B Using significant figures

You can find an approximate answer to the calculation $3{\cdot}17 \times 3{\cdot}83$ by rounding $3{\cdot}17$ and $3{\cdot}83$ to 1 significant figure.

This leaves the much simpler calculation 3×4 whose answer is 12.

B1 How close to 12 is the answer to $3{\cdot}17 \times 3{\cdot}83$?
Find out using a calculator.

B2 By rounding to 1 s.f. find an approximate answer to $31{\cdot}3 \div 4{\cdot}823$.
Find how close your approximate answer was to the exact one by using a calculator.

B3 Round to 1 s.f. to find an approximate answer to these.
Use a calculator to find how close your approximations are to the exact answers.

   (a) $47{\cdot}71 \times 13{\cdot}69$ (b) $112{\cdot}7 \times 4{\cdot}9$ (c) $60{\cdot}456 \times 5{\cdot}15$

   (d) $0{\cdot}95 \times 4{\cdot}9$ (e) $44{\cdot}567 \div 8{\cdot}06$

An investigation for two or more people

For this investigation you will need to share the tasks out.
Discuss your findings together and write a report.

The answer to $417{\cdot}2 \times 19$ is $7926{\cdot}8$ *(using a calculator)*
   $417{\cdot}2$ correct to 1 s.f. is 400.
   19 correct to 1 s.f. is 20.
   $400 \times 20 = 8000$, but 8000 is $7926{\cdot}8$ correct to 1 s.f.!

* Make up some multiplications of your own.
  Does rounding each number to 1 s.f. always give an answer correct to 1 s.f.?

* What about divisions, additions or subtractions?

* What happens if you round numbers to 2 s.f.?

Surveys – a review

Before carrying out a survey you must plan exactly what to do.
(Surveys carried out by large companies may cost thousands of pounds!)

You need to think about who to ask, what to ask and where to ask it.
Your questions also need to be easily understood.

Here are the details of some surveys.
Unfortunately the people who did them were not very careful!

For each one, say what you think is wrong with it, and how you would improve it.

1 Are you a vegetarian? | YES | | NO |

2 Do you think there should be more nursery schools in the district or should the money be spent on more sports facilities? | YES | | NO |

3 Tracey wanted to find out how pupils got to school in the morning.
She decided to ask 50 people in her year group at random in the playground at lunch time and designed this table to record her results.

Method	Tally	Total
Bus		
Bicycle		
Walk		

4 Thomas wants to find out what residents think of the plan to build a fish and chip shop on their housing estate.

> Do you think a smelly fish and chip shop should be built on the estate?
>
> YES | NO

5 Media Mags needed to find out which magazines people read. They decided to carry out a teleiphone survey.

They picked out 250 names chosen at random from a page of the phone book. These numbers were phoned up between midday and 2 p.m. Whoever answered the phone was asked what magazines they had read over the last week. These answers were collected, and put together in a table.

Type of magazine	Percentage
Pop music	6
Classical music	3
Puzzle magazines	30

6 Sanjay decided to do a survey on how much homework the pupils in his school did. He asked all his friends and kept a note of their replies. He wanted to show the results on a bar chart. Here are his raw results.

> 1 Usually about 15 minutes, but last night almost an hour.
>
> 2 I always do it at school.
>
> 3 Didn't do any last night.
>
> 4 Two hours at the weekend but less during the week.

7 A local sports centre wants to know what the people who use it think of the facilities. They ask users to fill in a six-page form before getting changed. The first question is:

> In general are you satisfied by the general level of in-house facilities offered at the above centre or should they be improved?
>
> YES | NO

6 It's getting better all the time

Think of a number

Work through these problems with a partner.

A1   I am thinking of a number.
I subtract 5.
The answer is 6.
What number am I thinking of?

A2   I am thinking of a number.
I add 23.
The answer is 37.
What number am I thinking of?

A3   I think of a number.
I multiply it by 10.
The answer is 60.
What number am I thinking of?

A4   I think of a number.
I divide it by 3.
The answer is 4.
What is the number?

A5   I think of a number.
I double it and add 5.
The answer is 11.
What is the number?

A6   Make up some more *I think of a number* type problems
for yourselves. Test them on each other.

A7   Look back at how you did the *I think of a number* problems.
Are there any simple rules you found to help you solve the
problems? Experiment for yourselves.
(You may need to check your rules by inventing *and solving*
some more problems.)

Phil found two ways of solving the problem in **A5**.
Read through each method together. Make sure
you understand each one.

Working backwards

$11 - 5 = 6$ *because subtracting 5*
                     'undoes' adding 5.
$6 \div 2 = 3$ *because dividing by 2*
                     'undoes' doubling.
So the number is 3.

Using algebra

Let x stand for the number.
$2x + 5 = 11$ *2 times x, add 5 is 11.*
$2x = 11 - 5$
$2x = 6$
$x = 3$
So the number is 3.

A8 Choose one of the other problems on page 33.
Use each of Phil's methods to solve it.

Another method that Phil could have used is **trial and improvement**.
He guesses a number, tries it and then adjusts this guess to produce a
new trial number.

Remember we are looking for a number which when doubled and five
is added to it gives eleven, or $2 \times \boxed{\text{number}} + 5 = 11$.

First try, **10**: $2 \times 10 + 5 = 25$ *too big*

Second try, **8**: $2 \times 8 + 5 = 21$ *too big*

Third try, **2**: $2 \times 2 + 5 = 9$ *too small*
So we know the answer (or solution) will be between 8 and 2.

Fourth try, **4**: $2 \times 4 + 5 = 13$ *too big*
So we know the number will be between 4 and 2.

Fifth try, **3**: $2 \times 3 + 5 = 11$
So the number is 3.

Use a method of your own choice to answer A9–A12.

A9 I think of a number, add 3 to it, then divide by 2.
The answer is 7. What is my number?

A10 I think of a number, subtract 4 from it, then divide by 3.
The answer is 4. What is my number?

A11 I think of a number, add 1 and square it.
The answer is 36. What is my number?

A12 I think of a number, divide it by 3 and square it.
The answer is 16. What is my number?

B Being methodical

If you had to solve the equation $3x + 2 = 14$, you could try different values of x then work out the value of the left-hand side and compare the result with 14.

For example,

x	$3x + 2$	
5	17	too big
1	5	too small
3	11	too small
4	14	correct

So the solution to the equation $3x + 2 = 14$ is $x = 4$.

But if the equation was $3x + 2 = 15$:

x	$3x + 2$	
4	14	too small
5	17	too big
4·5	15·5	too big
4·3	14·9	too small
4·4	15·2	too big

So the solution lies between 4·3 and 4·4.

4·35	15·05	too big
4·32	14·96	too small
4·34	15·02	too big
...	...	

You keep on **trying** and **improving** until you have an answer which you think is accurate enough.

In this example we know that the solution is between 4·32 and 4·34. Since the solution is less than 4·35 we know that 'The solution is 4·3 correct to 1 decimal place'.

B1 (a) What value does $3x + 2$ have when $x = 4·33$?

(b) Is this trial value of x too big or too small?

(c) What should the next trial value of x be?

Talking Point

Nina and Rose are solving an equation using trial and improvement. They find that a trial value for x of 3·747 is too small but one of 3·749 is too big.

Nina says that they have an accurate answer and should write the solution as 3·748 correct to 3 decimal places. Is she correct?
Discuss this with a partner and explain your answer to your teacher.

B2 Simian has started to solve the equation $7x - 3 = 50$.
Here is his working so far.

x	$7x - 3$	
7	46	too small
8	53	too big
7·5	49·5	too small
7·75	51·25	too big

Continue Simian's working to find a solution correct to
1 decimal place.

B3 Jackie has started to solve the equation $x^2 + 5x = 30$.
It was a little more complicated than Simian's, but the
method is exactly the same. Here is her working so far.

x	x^2	$5x$	$x^2 + 5x$	
4	16	20	36	too big
3	9	15	24	too small
3·5	12·25	17·5	29·75	too small
3·6	12·96	18	30·96	too big

Continue Jackie's working to find a solution correct to
2 decimal places.

B4 Solve the following equations using trial and improvement.
You will need to draw up tables like Simian's or Jackie's.
In each case give your answers correct to 2 decimal places.

(a) $3x - 4 = 9$ (b) $7x + 1 = 21$ (c) $x^2 = 20$

(d) $x^3 = 30$ (careful here!)   (e) $x^2 + x = 35$ (f) $x^2 - x = 50$

B5 When runners or walkers reach speeds
greater than v m/s, given by the
equation $v^2 = 10$, both their feet lose
contact with the ground.
Find by trial and improvement what
this speed is.

B6 The time taken, t, in seconds for a stone to fall s metres can be
worked out using the formula $s = 5t^2$.
The deepest well in Great Britain is 126 metres deep.
How long would it take a stone to fall this distance?
Decide for yourself how accurate your answer need be.

B7 The distance to the horizon, d km, is connected to the height,
h, in metres a person is above sea-level by the formula $d^2 = 13h$.
If you stand on a cliff 25 m high, how far away could you see a ship?
Decide for yourself how accurate your answer need be.

Circles – a review

In most reference books there are formulas for calculating the areas of shapes.

Circle	Parallelogram	Triangle
	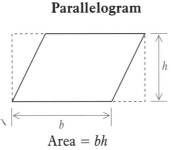	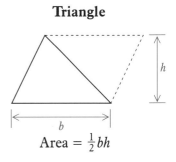
	Area = bh	Area = $\frac{1}{2}bh$

Circumference = $2\pi r = \pi d$

Area = $\pi r^2 = \frac{1}{4}\pi d^2$ (The value of π is approximately 3·14.)

1. What does h in the formulas for the parallelogram and triangle stand for?

2. In the formulas for the circle what do the letters r and d stand for?

3. Draw these shapes full size on centimetre squared paper.

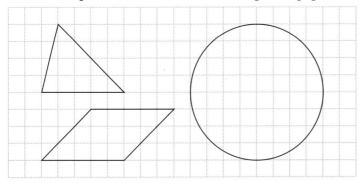

   (a) Find the area of each shape by counting squares.

   (b) Use the formulas to calculate the area of each shape.

   (c) Check your answers to (b) by comparing them with (a).

   (d) Try to find a way to measure the circumference (perimeter) of
      the circle. Compare your answer with the value found using the
      formula. How close were the two different values?

The formula for the area of a circle $\frac{1}{4}\pi d^2$ means (π divided by four)
multiplied by (the value of the diameter squared).

Check, by using this formula, that the area of a 10 cm diameter circle
is 78·5 cm². Take 3·14 as the value for π.

Use the formula involving the radius to find the area of the circle.
Check that it is 78·5 cm².

5

When you double the radius of a circle, you double its area.

No! When you double the radius the circumference is doubled.

Who (if either) is correct, Jerry or Amanda?
Give some actual figures to support your answer.

Talking Point

Many people from different parts of the world live in dwellings which have circular bases. For example, native Americans live in tepees, Mongols from Siberia in yurts and Inuits in igloos.

What advantages has the circle over the square or rectangle? Use figures to support your arguments.
(**Hint.** Look at areas and perimeters.)
Tell your teacher your reasons.

6 These two circles share the same centre. Circles which do this are called **concentric**.

(a) The gap is the distance between the two circles. Find a connection between the gap and the **diameters** of the concentric circles forming it. You may need to draw some concentric circles.

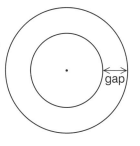

(b) Deborah says that the difference between the circumferences of two concentric circles is just twice the gap times π.

It does not depend on the diameters of either of the circles!
Is she right? Investigate some concentric circles for yourselves.

7 Find by trial and improvement the radius, to the nearest centimetre, of a circle which has an area of $10\,000\,\text{cm}^2$. Here is a start.

Radius (r)	Area (πr^2)	
10	$3.14 \times 100 = 314$	too small
100	$3.14 \times 10\,000 = 31\,400$	too large

7 Transforming shapes

A Reflection

The triangle ABC has been reflected
in the dotted line to give the
triangle A′B′C′.

We call the dotted line a **mirror line**.

The triangle ABC in its starting position
is called the **object** of the reflection.

The result of reflecting the object
is called the **image**.

We also use the words object and
image when talking about points.
For example, the point A is an
object and A′ its image.

When a letter is used to name a point,
then the image is usually shown by
using the same letter with a dash.

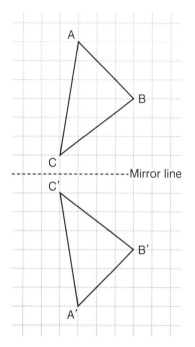

A1 Copy each of these diagrams and reflect the shape in the dotted
line. Don't forget to label the image of A as A′, B as B′, and so on.

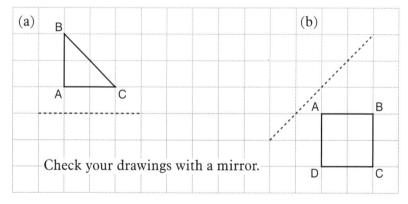

Check your drawings with a mirror.

A2 Look back at your answers to **A1**.
The lettering of the two objects is arranged
alphabetically in clockwise order.

Is this true for the images of the two shapes?

Experiment with some shapes of your own.
What do you find?

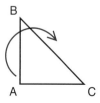

B Rotations of 180°

In this diagram the flag has been **rotated 180° clockwise** about the point C.

The point C is called the **centre of rotation**.

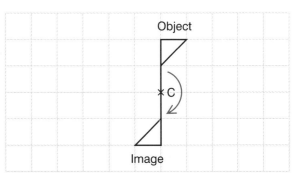

The centre of rotation does not have to be a point on the object itself. For example:

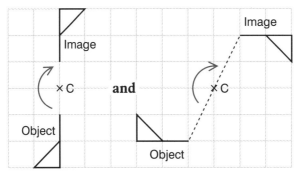

You can use a piece of tracing paper to find the position of an image after a 180° rotation (in this case a rotation *clockwise*).

This triangle is to be rotated through 180° clockwise about C.

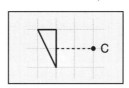

Trace the object and the centre of rotation.

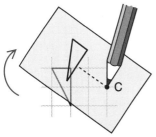

Then rotate the tracing clockwise keeping the point C fixed ...

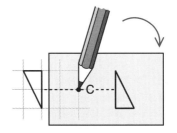

... until the tracing has been rotated through 180°. The tracing shows the position of the image.

B1–B3 These questions are on worksheet B+ 3.

C Rotations of 90°

This diagram shows how to use tracing paper to find the
image of an object after a 90° rotation **anticlockwise** about
the centre C.

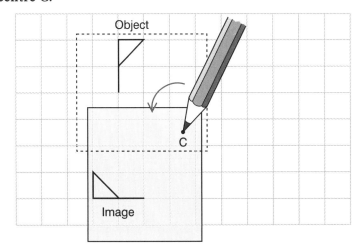

C1–C3   These questions are on worksheet B+ 4.

Sometimes it can be difficult to find the image of a point which
has been rotated. This method can be very useful.

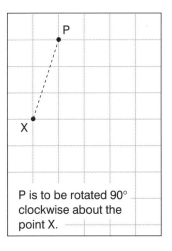

P is to be rotated 90°
clockwise about the
point X.

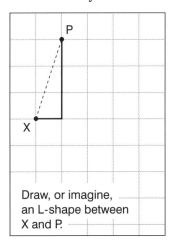

Draw, or imagine,
an L-shape between
X and P.

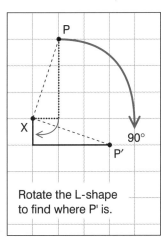

Rotate the L-shape
to find where P' is.

C4–C5   These questions are on worksheet B+ 5.

C6   A point P is rotated 90° clockwise about a point X to give
an image P'.
What anticlockwise rotation about X will have the same image?

D Coordinates, reflections and rotations

D1 Make a copy of this grid on squared paper.

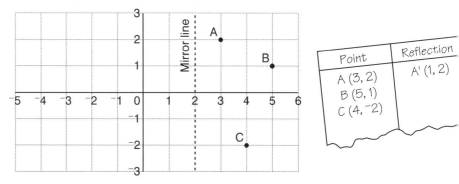

A is the point (3, 2). The image of A (A′) after it has been reflected in the mirror line is (1, 2).

(a) Find the coordinates of B and C after they have been reflected in the mirror line.

(b) Draw some more points on your grid together with their images after reflection in the mirror line.

(c) Look carefully at the coordinates of the points and their images. Can you find a relationship between them?

(d) Investigate the coordinates of the images of points for different vertical positions of the mirror line.
Make a note of anything interesting you find.

D2

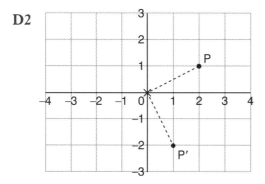

The point P (2, 1) has been rotated 90° clockwise about the point (0, to give its image P′ at (1, ⁻2).

(Another word for (0, 0) is the **origin**.)

Choose some other points and rotate them 90° clockwise about the origin. Try to find a connection between the coordinates of the object and image points.

What about rotations of 180° or 270° about the origin – clockwise and anticlockwise? Investigate these with a partner.

8 Pencil and paper 2

(a chapter for two people)

A Ways of looking at division

A1 Write down which of the calculations below fit each of these problems.

(a) Twelve divided by three.

(b) How many threes are there in twelve?

(c) Divide twelve by three.

(d) What does three need to be multiplied by to make twelve?

(e) Three divided by twelve.

(f) Share out £12 equally between three people.

(g) Share £3 equally between twelve people.

| 12 ÷ 3 | 3 ÷ 12 | 12 × 3 | 3 × 12 |

A2 Write a sentence which fits each of these calculations.

(a) 20 ÷ 4   (b) 4 ÷ 20

A3 What is the connection between the answer to the calculation 30 ÷ 6 and the number of times you can subtract six from thirty?

Experiment with some other divisions, like 20 ÷ 4, for yourselves. What do you notice?

A4 Write down at least six different divisions whose answer is five.

A5 (a) Look at these division patterns.

    (i) $20 \div 4 = 5$ (ii) $256 \div 64 = 4$

            $40 \div 8 = 5$ $128 \div 32 = 4$

            $80 \div 16 = 5$ $64 \div 16 = 4$

         $160 \div 32 = 5$ $32 \div 8 = 4$

Continue them for a few more divisions.

(b) Describe what is happening in (i) and (ii).

(c) Make up some division patterns like those in (i) and (ii). Note anything interesting.

A6 Here are some of Angela's calculations.
Look carefully at her working.
Use her method to answer (a), (b) and (c).

    $336 \div 48$ $828 \div 18$

    $168 \div 24$ $414 \div 9$

    $84 \div 12$ $138 \div 3 = 46$

    $42 \div 6 = 7$ so $828 \div 18 = 46$

so $336 \div 48 = 7$

(a) $648 \div 72$ (b) $448 \div 16$ (c) $864 \div 96$

A7 (a) If you know that $35 \div 5 = 7$, you can write down straight away that $35 \div 7 = 5$ and $7 \times 5 = 35$.
What can you write down straight away from $806 \div 26 = 31$?

(b) Use a calculator to find a 5-digit number which can be divided exactly by a 3-digit number.

A8 Angela says that a division can be checked by doing a multiplication.
Explain what Angela means. Some examples might help.

A9 Simon copied down this number trick.
But he accidentally tore off the last line giving the trick.

Write 37 on a piece of paper and keep it safe.
Ask someone to choose one of the digits 1–9.
Ask them to write down a 3-digit number made by repeating this digit.
Tell them to add together these three digits and divide the 3-digit number by the answer.
Whatever number they chose

What is missing?

A10 Without using a calculator, match these calculations with the calculator displays shown below.

(a) $18 \div 4$ (b) $450 \div 5$ (c) $100 \div 5$ (d) $45 \div 5$

(e) $209 \div 11$ (f) $45 \div 9$

A | `5`   B | `4.5`

C | `9`   D | `19`   E | `20`   F | `90`

A11 Working together, without using a calculator, find the value of the missing digit $*$ in each of these.

(a) $124 \div * = 31$ (b) $3*8 \div 8 = 41$

(c) $24* \div 4 = 62$ (d) $2*6 \div 6 = 36$

A12 Make up some puzzles like the ones in **A11**. Try them on each other.

B Take your pick

Here are some pencil-and-paper methods for division.
Look at each method together and use it to do the problems after each one.

B1 $208 \div 16$

```
  208        144        80
  -16        -16       -16
  192        128        64
  -16        -16       -16
  176        112        48
  -16        -16       -16
  160        112        32
  -16        -16       -16
  160        -16        16
             96        -16
             -16        16
             80        -16
                        00
```

16 can be taken from 208 thirteen times, so $208 \div 16 = 13$.

(a) A group of 37 students hires a coach to go to a pop concert.
The hire of the coach costs £259.
How much should each student pay?

(b) How many 17 cm lengths of string can be cut from a piece of string 119 cm long?

(c) Lorraine works out that she spends £168 a year on magazines. How much does she spend a month on magazines?

(d) A large 45-floor office block is 135 m tall. How high is a single floor?

B2 208 ÷ 16 is the same as asking how 208 can be divided equally between 16.

16 × **10** = 160

This leaves 208 − 160 = 48

16 × **3** = 48

So 208 shared equally between 16 is 13 (= 10 + 3).

(a) Michael saved up £676 over a year for a holiday.
On average how much did he save in a week?
There are 52 weeks in a year.

(b) On long journeys a car travels at an average speed of
46 miles per hour. At this speed how long would it take
to travel from London to Glasgow, a distance of 414 miles?

B3 This method was quite widely used in the 15th century. It only
works if you can split up the number you are dividing by.

So for 208 ÷ 16

$$16 = 2 × 8$$
$$So\ 208 ÷ 16 = (208 ÷ 2) ÷ 8$$
$$208 ÷ 2 = 104$$
$$104 ÷ 8 = 13$$

This means that   208 ÷ 16 = 13.

(a) Check that the method works for 208 ÷ 16 if you split up
16 into 4 × 4,   2 × 8   or   2 × 2 × 2 × 2.

(b)

A train breaks down and all 384 passengers need to be
taken to the next station by coach. Each coach can carry
48 passengers. How many full coach trips will be needed?

B4 The Ancient Egyptians would have worked out the division 208 ÷ 16 by asking 'How many times should 16 be added together to give 208?'

They would do the calculation like this.

First of all they would keep on doubling sixteen to find 2 × 16, 4 × 16, 8 × 16, etc.

$$1 \times 16 = 16$$
$$2 \times 16 = 32$$
$$4 \times 16 = 64$$
$$8 \times 16 = 128$$
$$16 \times 16 = 256$$
$$32 \times 16 = 512$$

Then they would look at the right-hand numbers to find which gave 208 when added together.

8 lots of 16 are 128, leaving 208 − 128 = 80, but
4 lots of 16 are 64.
This leaves 80 − 64 = 16 which is just **1 lot** of 16!
So   8 + 4 + 1 = 13 lots of 16 make 208
or   208 ÷ 16 = 13.

(a) How many £20 notes are needed to make a total of £720?

(b) A booklet is 468 lines long. There are 39 lines on a page. How many pages are there in the booklet?

(c) Graham finds there is a total of 528 matches in 11 matchboxes. What is the mean number of matches in a box?

B5 This method probably came from either Persian or Arab mathematicians.

$$\begin{array}{r} 13 \\ 16\overline{)20\overset{4}{8}} \end{array}$$

(a) In 1983 Norman Johnson, a catering student in Blackpool, cut a cucumber into 264 slices. The cucumber was 12 inches long. How many slices, on average, was each inch of cucumber cut into?

(b) One of the largest beetroots ever grown weighed 464 ounces. There are 16 ounces in a pound. How many pounds did the beetroot weigh?

47

C Left overs

Try to do C1–C6 without using a calculator.

C1 In the old money there were twelve pennies in a shilling.
Ajaz saved up 228 pennies.
How many shillings was this?

C2 In imperial measures fourteen pounds make a stone.
Bill weighs 210 pounds. How many stones is this?

C3

The average person weighs 70 kg. What is the maximum number of people of average weight who could travel in this lift?

C4 Not all divisions give a whole number answer.
There can sometimes be a remainder.
The calculation $160 \div 13$ has a remainder of 4.
Use some of the methods of division to calculate $160 \div 13$.
Which method is easiest for finding remainders?

C5 Janice is packing eggs into boxes. Each box contains 12 eggs.
She has to pack 500 eggs. How many boxes will these fill?
How many eggs are left over?

C6

I think of two whole numbers and divide one by the other. The remainder is 5.

What whole numbers can Joseph *not* have divided by?

9 3-D symmetries

You will need multilink cubes and a mirror.
You should ignore the holes and connectors.

A Reflection symmetry

1
Make these two shapes with
multilink cubes.

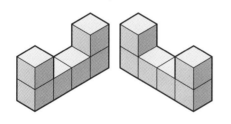

2
Put the two shapes side by side.
This makes a bigger shape.

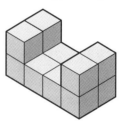

3
Now put a mirror in the middle of the big shape like this.

Take the mirror away, then put it back.
The big shape does not change.
One side is the reflection of the other.

We say the big shape has **reflection symmetry**.
The mirror is a **plane of symmetry**.

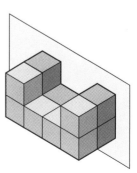

A1 Does the big shape have any other planes of symmetry?

Check with a mirror. (You will need to split the shape in two.)

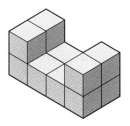

A2 Make this shape from 16 multilink cubes. How many planes of symmetry does it have?

Check your answers with someone else. (**Hint.** There is more than one plane of symmetry.)

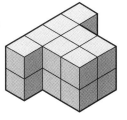

A3 How many planes of symmetry do each of these multilink models have? Check your answers with someone else.

(a)   (b) (c)

Talking Point

Angela says that this building has a plane of symmetry.

But Gemma says that in real life it would never have a true plane of symmetry.

Who is right?

A4 **This is a question for two to do.**
Below are some sketches of everyday objects.
Which of them have planes of symmetry?

For those that are symmetrical say how many planes of
symmetry there are.

For the ones which are not symmetrical write your reasons
for your answer.

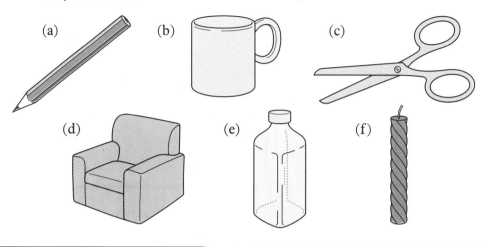

(a)   (b)   (c)

(d)   (e)   (f)

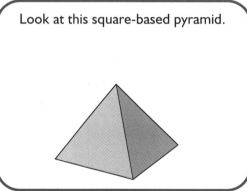

Look at this square-based pyramid.

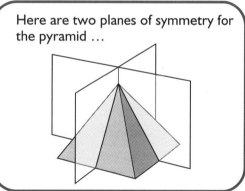

Here are two planes of symmetry for
the pyramid …

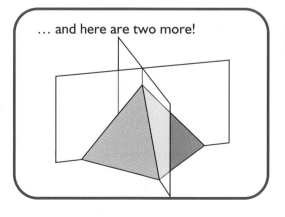

… and here are two more!

Altogether the square-based pyramid
has four planes of symmetry.

A5 This solid is a square-based pyramid with a cube fitted underneath it.

How many planes of symmetry does the solid have?

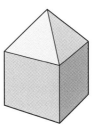

A6 Here are some solid shapes.
How many planes of symmetry does each of them have?

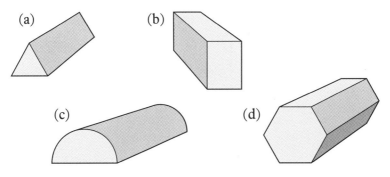

(a)

(b)

(c)

(d)

A7 Make a shape from five multilink cubes that has no planes of symmetry.

A8 Make shapes from six multilink cubes which have exactly these numbers of planes of symmetry:

(a) zero   (b) one   (c) two

(d) three   (e) four   (f) five

A9

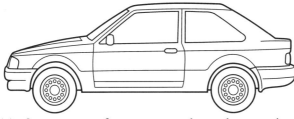

(a) Some parts of a car are made so that one is a reflection (mirror image) of the other, for example, the car wings.
Name some other parts which are mirror images of each other.

(b) The driver's door is damaged.
Can it be replaced with a passenger's door?
Give a reason for your answer.

B Rotation symmetry

Make this shape from multilink cubes.

Put the cubes together so that a pencil
will fit down the middle.

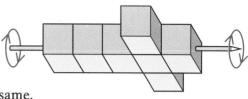

Rotate the shape round the pencil.
There are two positions where it looks the same.

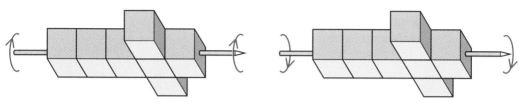

The line of the pencil is called an **axis of rotation symmetry**.
We say that this shape has **rotation symmetry of order 2** about the axis
or line of the pencil.

B1 Add one more cube to your shape to make this.
Does your new shape have rotation symmetry?

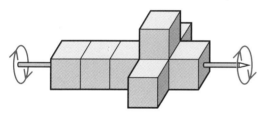

B2 Add another cube to make this shape. What is the order of
rotation symmetry of the shape about the pencil now?

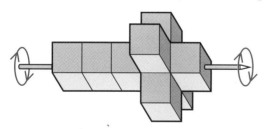

B3 Add 4 more cubes to make
this shape.
What is the order of rotation
symmetry about the pencil now?

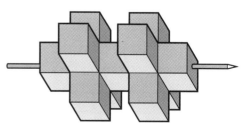

B4 Imagine you could stick a pencil through the shape like this.

What is the order of rotation symmetry about this axis?

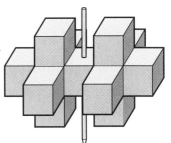

B5 (a) What is the order of rotation symmetry of this shape about axis A?

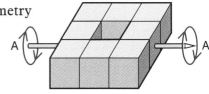

(b) What is the order of rotation symmetry of the shape about axis B?

(c) Find another axis of rotation symmetry for this shape.

Sketch the shape showing where you could put your axis of symmetry.

Can you find any more?

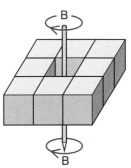

B6 Each of these solid shapes has rotation symmetry about the axis shown.
What is the order of rotation symmetry of each shape?

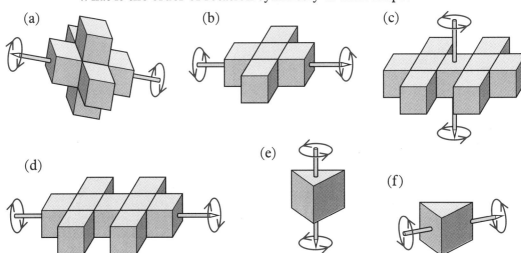

(a)

(b)

(c)

(d)

(e)

(f)

B7 This solid has rotation symmetry of order 2.

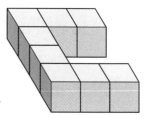

(a) Sketch it and show the position of its axis of symmetry.

(b) Arrange 8 multilink cubes to make another solid which has rotation symmetry of order 4. Sketch this new solid.

B8 Using just 7 multilink cubes, make a solid which has rotation symmetry of order 2, but no planes of symmetry.

B9 **This is a question for two people to discuss together.**
Some of these shapes have rotation symmetry.
For each one say whether or not it has rotation symmetry.
Give a reason for your answer.
This may depend on what you think the solid is like in real life.

(a)

(b)

(c)

(d)

(e)

(f)

(g)

(h)

10 Negative numbers

(a chapter for two people)

A Plus, minus, add and subtract

For most of this chapter you will need a calculator with a $\boxed{+/-}$ key.

Most people find working with negative numbers difficult at first.
This is probably because the '–' symbol can mean two different things!

Negative two (⁻2)

⁻2 is a number marked on the number line or a point on a scale.

This is the point
negative two.

For example, the temperature ⁻2°C (negative two degrees Celsius):

Temperature °C

Minus two (– 2)

– 2 tells you to subtract two, for example, 7 – 2 = 5.

It only means something when another number is involved.

Talking Points

In each of these examples, decide which of these meanings
the symbol '–' has.

- The temperature in Chicago was ⁻10°C.

- ⁻5 + ⁻5 = ⁻10   3 – 4 = ⁻1   ⁻6 is less than ⁻1.

One way to display negative (**not** minus) two on your calculator is to use it to calculate 'two *minus* four'.

A1 How does your calculator display negative five?
Check your answer by using your calculator to work out negative five add five.
The display should show zero. Why?

A2 Investigate what the $\boxed{+/-}$ key does by doing calculations like these.

Number stands for any number you want to key in.

number + number $\boxed{+/-}$ $\boxed{=}$

or $\boxed{\text{number}}$ $\boxed{+/-}$ + $\boxed{\text{number}}$ $\boxed{+/-}$ $\boxed{=}$

or $\boxed{\text{number}}$ $\boxed{+/-}$ $\boxed{+/-}$ + $\boxed{\text{number}}$ $\boxed{+/-}$ $\boxed{=}$

Experiment for yourselves.

Write a few sentences explaining what the $\boxed{+/-}$ key does.

A3 Write down these calculations in numbers and work them out.

(a) Six minus ten

(b) Ten minus six

(c) Four add negative one

(d) Negative one add four and a half

A4 Use your calculator to work these out.

(a) $2 + {}^-2$ (b) ${}^-2 + 2$ (c) ${}^-2 + {}^-2$

(d) ${}^-5 + {}^-5$ (e) $5 + {}^-5$ (f) $0 + {}^-3$

(g) $2 + {}^-1 \cdot 5$ (h) ${}^-1\frac{1}{2} + {}^-1\frac{1}{2}$

${}^-5 + {}^-8$ and $3 + 7$ are both called **expressions**.
The first expression has a value of ${}^-13$ and the second has a value of 10.

Question **A4** should perhaps have said:
'Work out the values of these expressions'.

A5 Write down some different expressions with values of:

(a) zero   (b) ${}^-5$ (c) 5

Try to make your expressions quite complicated, but make sure they give the correct values when you work them out (evaluate them).

A6 Use your calculator to investigate and extend these number patterns. Write down anything interesting that you notice.

(a) $3 - 2 = 1$ (Three minus two gives one.)
$3 - 1 = 2$
$3 - 0 = 3$
$3 - {}^-1 =$
$3 - {}^-2 =$
$3 - {}^-3 =$

(b) $3 - {}^-2 = 5$ (Three minus negative two gives five.)
$3 - {}^-1 = 4$
$3 - 0 =$
$3 - 1 =$
$3 - 2 =$

(c) $3 + {}^-2 = 1$ (Three plus negative two gives one.)
$3 + {}^-1 =$
$3 + 0 =$
$3 + 1 =$
$3 + 2 =$

A7 Read these three statements carefully.
Check which of them are true by making up your own calculations.
You may find some of the answers to **A6** useful.

(a) Subtracting a positive number is the same as adding the negative value of the same number.
e.g. $10 - 4$ has the same value as $10 + {}^-4$.

(b) Subtracting a negative number is the same as adding the positive value of the same number.
e.g. $20 - {}^-5$ has the same value as $20 + 5$.

(c) Adding a negative number is the same as subtracting the positive value of the same number.
e.g. $20 + {}^-4$ has the same value as $20 - 4$.

A8 During the 'day' the temperature on the moon can reach $110\,°C$ but at 'night' it drops to $^-155\,°C$. Which of the calculations gives the difference between these two temperatures?

$^-110 - {}^-155 = 45$

$^-155 - {}^-110 = {}^-45$

$155 - 110 = 45$

$110 - {}^-155 = 265$

58

A9 In a magic square the sum of the numbers in a row, column or diagonal are the same. This is called the magic number. Here is a magic square involving some negative numbers.

⁻3	2	1
4	0	⁻4
⁻1	⁻2	3

Check that the square is magic and that the magic number is zero.

A10 Copy and complete these magic squares.
In each case work out the magic number.

(a)
0	5	
	1	3
4		2

(b)
	8	⁻6
	0	4
6		

(c)
	⁻5	2
1		
⁻4	3	⁻2

A11 Choose one or more of the magic squares above.
Investigate what happens when you *subtract* the same number from each of the numbers in the magic square.

Does the magic number alter?
If it does, how? Try to find some rules.

What happens when you *add* the same number to all the numbers?

A12 A subtraction (or addition) can be checked by using an addition (or subtraction). For example:

> Look at 10 – 2.
>
> If 8 is the correct answer then 8 + 2 should give 10.
> Which it *does!*
>
> If 6 + 3 is equal to 9 then 9 – 3 should give 6.
> Which it *does!*

(a) Can you explain why these checks work?
   (**Hint.** Think about equations.)

(b) Does these checks work for negative numbers?
   Investigate for yourselves.

B Multiplication and division with negative numbers

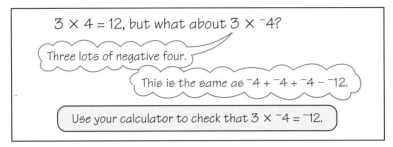

3 × 4 = 12, but what about 3 × ⁻4?

Three lots of negative four.

This is the same as ⁻4 + ⁻4 + ⁻4 − ⁻12.

Use your calculator to check that 3 × ⁻4 = ⁻12.

B1 Copy and complete this multiplication grid.
(**Hint**. Look for patterns.)

×	2	1	0	⁻1	⁻2
2	4	2	0	⁻2	⁻4
1	2	1	0	⁻1	⁻2
0	0	0	0	0	0
⁻1			0		
⁻2			0		

B2 Use any patterns you have noticed in **B1** to help you answer
these. Don't use a calculator.

(a) 3 × ⁻3   (b) ⁻4 × 3   (c) ⁻4 × ⁻3   (d) 10 × ⁻2

(e) ⁻6 × 4   (f) 4 × ⁻6   (g) ⁻4 × 6   (h) ⁻6 × ⁻4

Use a calculator to check your answers.

B3 Investigate this statement.
Write a short report of anything interesting you notice.

Multiplying with negative numbers is easy.
To find the number part just forget about the signs.

So, ignoring the sign, negative five multiplied by six is thirty.
The hard bit is finding the correct sign.

There does not seem to be a simple rule.

B4 Test any rules you both found in **B3** by trying at least three
of each of these types of multiplication:

(a) two negative numbers multiplied together

(b) a positive number multiplying a negative number

(c) a negative number multiplying a positive number

You may need to alter your rules!

B5 Make sure that both of you can answer questions like these without using a calculator.

(a) $^-4 \times {}^-5$ (b) $^-20 \times {}^-1$ (c) $15 \times {}^-2$ (d) $^-3 \times 20$

Check your answers with a calculator.

B6 Are these true or false?

(a) There is only one number which gives 100 when it is squared. It is 10.

(b) There is only one number which gives 1000 when it is cubed. It is 10.

Multiplication grids can also be used to help work out divisions.

For example, here is how to work out $^-6 \div {}^-2$ using a multiplication grid.

Make sure that you can see why it works.

×	3	2	1	0	$^-1$	$^-2$	$^-3$
3	9	6	3	0	$^-3$	$^-6$	$^-9$
2	6	4	2	0	$^-2$	$^-4$	$^-6$
1	3	2	1	0	$^-1$	$^-2$	$^-3$
0	0	0	0	0	0	0	0
$^-1$	$^-3$	$^-2$	$^-1$	0	1	2	3
$^-2$	$^-6$	$^-4$	$^-2$	0	2	4	6
$^-3$	$^-9$	$^-6$	$^-3$	0	3	6	9

$3 \times {}^-2 = {}^-6$
so $^-6 \div {}^-2 = 3$
(By using the grid backwards, $^-6 \div {}^-2$ is the same as asking what you multiply $^-2$ by to get $^-6$.)

B7 Use the multiplication grid above to answer these.

(a) $4 \div {}^-2$ (b) $^-4 \div 2$ (c) $^-9 \div {}^-3$

(d) $6 \div {}^-1$ (e) $^-6 \div 1$ (f) $^-2 \div {}^-1$

Check your answers using a calculator.
Can you see any patterns similar to those for multiplication?

B8 If $a = 3, b = {}^-3, c = 4$ and $d = {}^-1$, find the values of:

(a) $a + b$ (b) $a - c$ (c) ab (d) ^-b (e) bd

(f) da (g) ^-c (h) abc (i) $2b$ (j) ^-2c

11 Quadrilaterals

(a chapter for two people)

A Be precise!

Here is an excerpt from a mathematical dictionary.
It gives a definition and some **properties** of a rhombus.

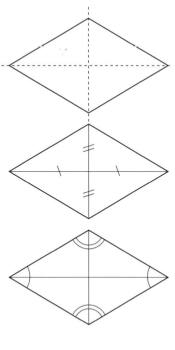

A rhombus is a quadrilateral (a shape with four sides.)

A rhombus has the following properties:

- two lines of symmetry (its diagonals)
- rotation symmetry of order two
- opposite sides parallel
- opposite angles equal
- diagonals bisecting each other at right-angles
- diagonals bisecting its angles

Chris says that a better definition of a rhombus is 'a quadrilateral which has four equal sides'. Is he right?

A1 Choose one of these shapes each.

square   rectangle

Write a definition of it which is as short as possible, together with a list of its properties.
Check each other's definition and list of properties.

Talking Point

Is a square a rectangle? Can a rectangle be a square?

Here are some quadrilaterals and their names.

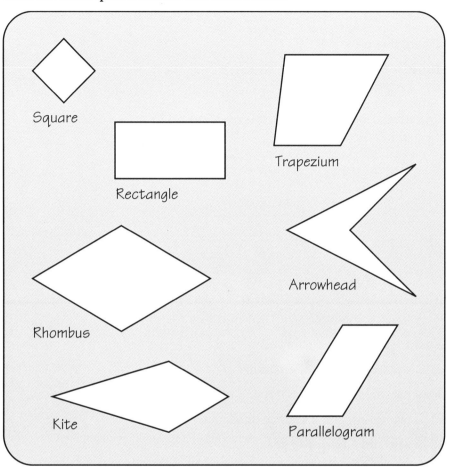

A2 There is another type of quadrilateral called a **scalene quadrilateral**. What do you think is special about this? [**Hint.** Remember scalene triangles?]

A3 Angles which are greater than 180° are called **reflex** angles. These marked internal angles are all reflex angles.

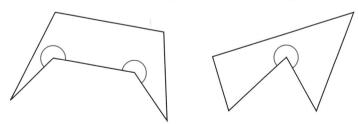

(a) What quadrilaterals (if any) have a reflex internal angle?

(b) Explain why it is impossible for a quadrilateral to have two internal angles which are reflex.

A4 This question is on worksheet B+ 6.

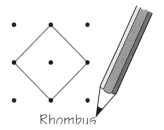

Rhombus

A5 Darren was classifying some quadrilaterals he had drawn for **A4**.

He wrote 'rhombus'. Was he correct? Give a reason for your answer.

A6 Find names for these quadrilaterals. They all have two pairs of equal parallel sides.

	Number of right-angles	Number of lines of symmetry
(a)	0	0
(b)	4	2
(c)	0	2
(d)	4	4

A7 What is the difference between:

(a) a square and a parallelogram?

(b) a parallelogram and a trapezium?

(c) a trapezium and a scalene quadrilateral?

(d) a kite and an arrowhead?

A8 Both of you should work together on this question.
You will need to discuss each other's ideas.
Here are five definitions of a kite.

> A kite is a quadrilateral which has:
> - perpendicular diagonals
> - at least one line of symmetry
> - a line of symmetry along one diagonal
> - a pair of equal length sides next to each other
> - one diagonal which bisects the other at right-angles

See for yourselves which other shapes satisfy some of these definitions.
Do all kites satisfy all of them?
How good are these definitions of a kite?
Try to improve on them yourselves.

B Odds and ends

Choose one of these to investigate for yourselves.

B1 Draw these rectangles; the areas are measured in cm² and the perimeters in cm.

(a) One having the same number for its area as its perimeter.

(b) One whose area number is twice the number of its perimeter.

B2 Kerry draws a quadrilateral.

She notices that if she marks the mid-points of the four sides and joins them up, she gets a rectangle.

Investigate whether this result is true for all quadrilaterals.

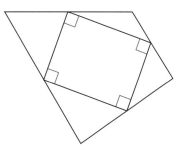

B3 Is it possible to work out whether a quadrilateral is a square just by looking at the coordinates of its corners?

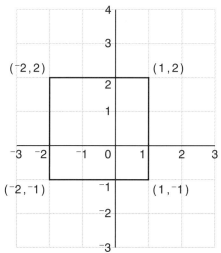

Make a note of anything interesting you find.

B4 Investigate some properties which might be used to classify quadrilaterals. You could try:

    number of lines of symmetry

    order of rotation symmetry

    how the diagonals cut each other

    your own ideas …

B5 Find as many properties of arrowheads as you can.

Number – a review

Factor
The factors of a number are those numbers which divide exactly into it. The factors of 20 are 1, 2, 4, 5, 10 and 20.

Divisible
The number 24 is divisible by 24, 12, 8, 6, 4, 3, 2 and 1 (They all divide exactly into 24.)

Prime number
A prime number has only two factors, itself and 1. 2, 3 and 13 are all prime numbers, but 1 is not.

Prime factor
The prime factors of 24 are 2 and 3.

Multiple
The numbers 3, 6, 9, 12 and 15 are all multiples of 3. This is because 3 is a factor of each of them.

Square root
The square root of 16 is 4 because 4×4 (4 squared) is 16. We write $\sqrt{16} = 4$.

Cube
Four cubed is $4 \times 4 \times 4 = 64$. This is sometimes written as 4

Cube root
The cube root of 8 is 2 because $2 \times 2 \times 2 = 8$; the cube root of 125 is 5 because $5 \times 5 \times 5 = 125$.

1 Is this true or false?
   The square root of a number is always less than the number itself.
   Give some examples to back up your answer.

2 Which three consecutive numbers multiplied together give 210?

3 The rule for a sequence is 'halve the previous term and add 2'.

   When the first term is 1, the sequence is 1,   2·5,   3·25,   3·625,   ...

   (a) Find the first four terms of the sequence when the first term is 4.

   (b) Investigate the sequence which begins with 1 and is generated by the rule 'halve the previous term and subtract it from 3'.

4 For each of these number patterns, try to write down the next two expressions in the pattern by looking at the previous ones.
   Check your answers with a calculator.

   (a) $\dfrac{1 \times 1}{1} = 1$ $\dfrac{22 \times 22}{1 + 2 + 1} = 121$ $\dfrac{333 \times 333}{1 + 2 + 3 + 2 + 1} = 12\,321$

   (b) $1 \times 2 \times 3 \times 4 + 1 = 5^2$
        $2 \times 3 \times 4 \times 5 + 1 = 11^2$
        $3 \times 4 \times 5 \times 6 + 1 = 19^2$

   (c) $1^3 = 1^2$
        $2^3 = (1 + 2)^2 - 1^2$
        $3^3 = (1 + 2 + 3)^2 - (1 + 2)^2$

5 Give some examples which make this clearer and easier to understand.
   Write down a 2-digit number. The difference between it and the number formed by interchanging the digits can be found by multiplying the difference between the two digits by nine.

6 Prime numbers which follow on from each other are called twin primes. For example, 5 and 7 are twin primes and so are 71 and 73.

  (a) How many twin primes can you find between 1 and 100?

  (b) Investigate one of these:
    (i) Add any two twin primes. Keep on adding the digits until you end up with just one digit. For example:
      $269 + 271 = 540 \rightarrow 5 + 4 + 0 = \mathbf{9}$
      and
      $461 + 463 = 924 \rightarrow 9 + 2 + 4 = 15 \rightarrow 1 + 5 = \mathbf{6}$
    (ii) Do the same as for (i) but start by multiplying the twin primes. For example:
      $269 \times 271 = 72\,899 \rightarrow 7 + 2 + 8 + 9 + 9 = 35 \rightarrow 3 + 5 = \mathbf{8}$

7 How can you tell if a number is divisible by five?

8 Are these true or false?

  (a) Multiples of nine can end in any of the ten digits.

  (b) Multiples of four always end in a 4, 6 or 8.

  (c) Multiples of three can end in any of the ten digits.

9 Find by trial and improvement the cube root of 2197.

10 This experiment lets you work out your reaction time in seconds.

You need a ruler marked in centimetres. Ask a friend to hold the ruler like this with the '0 cm' mark at the bottom.

Without touching the ruler, place your thumb and forefinger at the '0 cm' mark.

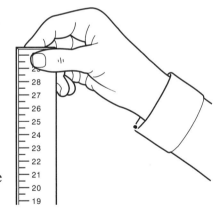

Your friend lets the ruler go without warning. As soon as the ruler falls, catch it and note where your thumb and forefinger have caught it. Call this distance x cm.

You can work out your reaction time (t seconds) using the formula
  $t = \sqrt{(0{\cdot}002x)}$.
Does your reaction time improve with practice?
What is your mean reaction time (correct to two decimal places) for ten tries?

11 Is this true or false?
Any number greater than 1 is either prime or the sum of two prime numbers.

12 Can you use all the digits from 1 to 9 (using each only once) to make five 1-digit and 2-digit prime numbers?

12 Revisiting equations

A What's it all about?

The expression $10 + (3 \times 4) - 2$ has the value $(10 + 12 - 2)$ which is 20.

10, (3×4) and 2 are called the **terms** of the expression.

An expression can also involve letters.

For example, $6x + 6$ is an expression and
$6x$ and 6 are each terms of the expression.

A1 The value of the expression $32 - 8 + (20 \div 5)$ is
$32 - 8 + 4 = 28$.

(a) The terms of the expression are 32, 8 and 4.
Double each term in the expression.
What is the new value of the expression?

(b) What happens to the value of the expression if all the terms are halved?

A2 Here are two expressions:

$14 + 16$ and $20 + 40 - 30$

The value of each expression is 30.

Investigate what happens to the value of each expression if:

(a) all the terms have one added to them   **e.g.** $(14 + 1) + (16 + 1)$

(b) all the terms are doubled   **e.g.** $(2 \times 20) + (2 \times 40) - (2 \times 30)$

(c) each expression has one added to it   **e.g.** $14 + 16 + 1$

A3 Write down two expressions which have a value of ten.
One of your expressions should have two terms and the other at least three terms.

(a) Choose a number. What happens to the value of your expressions when each term is

(i) multiplied   (ii) divided by this number?

(b) Investigate what happens to the value of each expression when your chosen number is

(i) added to   (ii) subtracted from each term.

Write a short report mentioning any rules you found.
Test your rules on some of your own expressions.

When you solve the equation $3x - 1 = x + 1$ you are trying to find the value of x which will make *the expression $3x - 1$* equal to *the expression $x + 1$*.

A4 What are the values of $3x - 1$ and $x + 1$ when the value of x is

(a) 0   (b) 1   (c) 2?

(d) Use your answers to write down the solution to the equation $3x - 1 = x + 1$.

A5 Here is what Sadia wrote in her notebook.

An equation shows that two expressions are equal.
When you solve an equation you need to find the value of the **unknown** (which is usually a letter) which fits the equation. This means it will make both these expressions have the same value.

You keep the expressions equal by treating them in the same way until you find this value.

Do you agree with what she has written?

A6 To back up her explanation Sadia showed how to solve some equations. Check her working in each of them.
Can you find any mistakes?

(1) $4x - 2 = 2x + 6$
$4x = 2x + 8$ (adding 2 to each expression)
$2x = 8$ (taking $2x$ from each expression)
$x = 2$

(2) $2x + 4 = x + 24$
$2x = x + 28$ (taking 4 from each expression)
$x = 28$ (taking x from each expression)

(3) $3x + 5 = 5x + 15$
$3x = 5x + 10$ (taking 5 from each expression)
$2x = 10$ (taking $3x$ from each expression)
$x = 5$

A7 Richard says the solution to $\dfrac{3x}{4} + 3 = x + 1$ is $x = 4$.

Jen says it is $x = 8$.

Find out who is right *without* solving the equation.

B Equations and formulas

B1 What value of a will make the expression $4a + 3$ equal to the expression $a + 9$?

B2 What value should x take in the expression $x^2 - 4$ so that the value of the expression is zero?

(**Challenge.** In fact it can take two values. Can you find the other one?)

B3 Solve each of these equations.
Show all the steps in your working so that someone else can follow exactly what you did.

Check your answers by finding out if both the right-hand and left-hand expressions are equal for your value of the **unknown** (the letter) in the equation.

(a) $10x - 10 = 0$ (b) $5s - 10 = 5$ (c) $6z + 4 = 3z +$

(d) $4{\cdot}5x - 1 = 2{\cdot}5x + 5$ (e) $5 = 10 - 5r$ (f) $4 + 3n = 4n +$

(g) $x + 9 = 3x + 2$ (h) $5 + 1{\cdot}5s = 9 + s$ (i) $50x = 5$

B4 A mountain stream is 20 cm deep. In spring, ice at the top of the mountain begins to melt and the water in the stream gets deeper.

The formula for the depth of the stream is $d = 11t + 20$, where d is the depth in centimetres of the stream and t is the time in days since the ice started to melt.

(a) Work out the depth of the stream after two days.

(b) If d is 53, what is t?

(c) If d is 75, what is t?

(d) When the stream has a depth of 97 cm, all the ice has melted. For how many days was the ice melting?

Now the water level starts to go down. The formula for the depth of water is $d = 97 - 17t$, where d is the stream depth in centimetres and t the number of days since the water started to go down.

(e) How long, to the nearest day, does it take the stream to return to its original depth of 20 cm?

B5 According to American psychologists the number of words, n, a child can understand depends on its age a in months and is given by the formula $n = 60a - 900$.

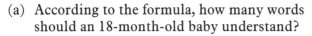

(a) According to the formula, how many words should an 18-month-old baby understand?

(b) Amil understands roughly 300 words. About how many months old is he?

(c) Will the formula work for very young children? Give reasons for your answer.

B6 Biologists have found that the number of chirps a cricket makes a minute is related to the temperature.

The formula which shows this is $t = 0{\cdot}6n$, where t is the temperature in °C and n the number of chirps the cricket makes in a minute.

(a) How many chirps each minute does a cricket make at 30°C?

(b) What does the formula predict will happen at very low temperatures? Does this seem reasonable?

B7 Some formulas don't work (are **not valid**) for certain values put (**substituted**) into them.

Authors of text books and teachers sometimes need to know the reading age of their books. One formula used to calculate this is $r = 25 - \dfrac{n}{10}$, where r is the reading age in years and n the number of one-syllable words in a 150-word passage.

For what reading ages is the formula useful?
(Use a dictionary or ask your teacher if you are not sure what a syllable is.)

B8 Jigsaw puzzles are usually easier if you do the edge pieces first. For a jigsaw puzzle which has l pieces in one direction and w pieces in the other, the percentage of edge pieces is $\dfrac{100(2l + 2w - 4)}{lw}$.

For example, a small 100-piece puzzle, 10 pieces by 10 pieces, has $l = w = 10$ and 36% of edge pieces.

(a) A 400-piece jigsaw is 20 pieces by 20 pieces. What percentage of the pieces are edge pieces?

(b) What percentage of the pieces are edge pieces in a 40 by 10 puzzle?

(c) Compare your answers to (a) and (b). Do they seem reasonable?

An equation generator

- Cut up ten pieces of paper.
- On each one of them write down a different expression involving numbers and x's.
- Try these first.

$x + 11$	$2x - 1$	$3 + 2x$	$x + 3$	$1 + x$

$6 + x$	$3x + 5$	$4x + 3$	$2x + 5$	$x - 6$

- Shuffle the pieces of paper.
- Pick up two at random.
- Take one as the left-hand side of an equation and the other as the right-hand side.
- Make a note of this equation.
- Try to solve the equation – don't forget to check your solution!
- Keep a record of your equations and whether they can be solved.
- When you have used all 10 pieces of paper, look back at the ones you could not solve.
- Is there anything special about these?

You will find discussing this with a partner useful.
You may need to make up some more equations to test your findings.

Formulas for equations – a challenge

Fatima wants to use her computer to solve equations.
Unfortunately, computers have to be told what to do!
So first she had to write the formula for solving an equation.
She decided to investigate equations like $6x + 4 = 10$ and $2x + 2 = 5$.

These all look like $ax + b = c$, where a, b and c stand for numbers in the equation.

Fatima wrote this down:

$$ax + b = c$$
$$ax = c - b \quad \text{(taking } b \text{ from both expressions)}$$
$$x = \frac{c - b}{a} \quad \text{(dividing both expressions by } a\text{)}$$

This was the formula she decided to use. Check to see if it works with some equations like $6x + 4 = 10$, $2x - 2 = 5$ and $5 - 2x = 3$.
Experiment for yourselves.

Super challenge – what about equations like $6x + 4 = 34 + x$?

13 Expressions with letters

A Expressions

Here are some examples of the number machine chain $\boxed{\times 2}$$\boxed{+1}$ $\longrightarrow$ in use.

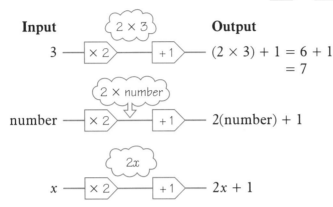

A1 Write down the output produced by $\boxed{\times 2}$$\boxed{+1}$ $\longrightarrow$ for these inputs.

(a) 4   (b) 6   (c) a (d) d

The number machine chain gives an output of $(2 \times 3) + 1$ for an input of 3.
We call $(2 \times 3) + 1$ an **expression** for the output. It has a value of 7.

A2 Write down the values of these expressions.

(a) $(4 \times 1) + 4$ (b) $(3 \times 2) + 4 - 10$

(c) $(3 \times 2) + (2 \times 2)$ (d) $4(2 + 8)$

A complete expression can be keyed into some calculators or a computer.

For example, with a graphical calculator:
Pressing $\boxed{\text{AC}}$ (on most calculators) clears the memory.
Then key in $(3 \times 6) + 8$, the expression to be evaluated.
Pressing $\boxed{\text{EXE}}$ will work out (evaluate) it and display 26.

To evaluate the same expression using BASIC or LOGO you need to
key in PRINT (3*6)+8 (Keyboards use * as the symbol for
multiplication.)

With BASIC and LOGO, if you want to evaluate $3(2 + 5)$ (which is 21)
you need to key in the multiplication symbol in front of the brackets:
   $3*(2 + 5)$
With most graphical calculators you don't need to do this.

A3 Use a graphical calculator, BASIC or LOGO to check your answers to **A2**.

A4 For each part write down three expressions with the value:

(a) 4   (b) 0   (c) ¯1   (d) 0·5

A5 Which of these expressions has the smallest value?

$20 \div 4$ $4 \div 20$ $2 + 4 + 3 - 1 - 1 - 2$ $(4 \times 3) - (1 \times 2)$ $3(2 - 1)$

Expressions can also involve letters. They are called **algebraic** expressions.

$2x + x + 4x - 2x$ $a + 2b + 3c + 6b - a$ $(a + b)$

Talking Point

How could you convince someone that these three expressions all have a value of $2x$?

$4x + 5x - 7x$ $4 + x - .4 + x$ $¯x + 3x + 2b + x - 2b - x$

A6 Try to match these sentences with some of the expressions below:

(a) Five lots of x (b) The product of x and y

(c) The difference between $4x$ and $2x$ (d) The sum of $4x$ and x

(e) Three lots of x plus y

(A) $3x + y$ (B) $4x + x$ (C) $3(x + y)$ (D) $5x$

(E) $x + y$ (F) $4x - 2x$ (G) xy

Challenge

Here are a BASIC program and a LOGO procedure.
Choose one of them and answer these.

What output would you expect with an input of 1·1 if you ran the program/procedure?

Try some other inputs. Write down what you would expect the outputs to be and check them by running the program/procedure.
Investigate what happens when you alter the expression in bold.

```
10 INPUT X
20 PRINT 2*X + X + 5*X
```

```
TO PUZZLE "X
PRINT 2*: X + :X + 5*:X
END
```

Magic?

B1 Follow through these instructions, choosing different starting numbers each time. What do you notice?

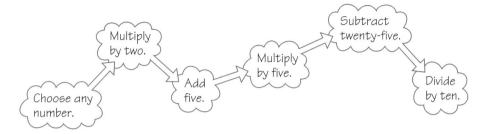

B2 Investigate the results of following these sets of instructions.

(a) • Choose any number.
   • Add the number one larger than your original choice.
   • Add eleven.
   • Divide by two.
   • Subtract the original number you chose.

(b) • Choose any number.
   • Multiply by three.
   • Add eight.
   • Add your starting number.
   • Divide by four.
   • Subtract your starting number.

(c) • Choose any number.
   • Multiply it by two.
   • Add nine.
   • Add the original number.
   • Divide by three.
   • Subtract three.

B3 How will your answers to **B1** and **B2** be affected if you choose decimals as starting numbers?

'Choose any number' problems like the ones on the last page always *seem* to give either the starting number or another number.

It does not seem to matter which starting number you choose.

But how can we be sure that this is true for all starting numbers?

Here is one way. We just call the starting number 'number' and see what happens.

Instruction	Example	Any 'number'
Choose any number	10	number
Multiply it by two	2 × 10	2(number) [Same as 2 × number]
Add five	2 × 10 + 5	2(number) + 5
Multiply by five	10 × 10 + 25	10(number) + 25 [Look at the example]
Subtract twenty-five	10 × 10	10(number) [Same as 10 × number]
Divide by ten	10	number [Back to the start!]

We did not say there was anything special about the 'number', so the result must be true for any number.

B4 Write down the missing entries in a copy of this table for **B2**(b).

Instruction	Example	Any 'number'
Choose any number	10	number
Multiply it by three	3 × 10	
Add eight	3 × 10 + 8	
Add the starting number	3 × 10 + 8 + 10 = 4 × 10 + 8	
Divide by four	10 + 2	
Subtract the starting number	2	

B5 Choose one of the other parts of **B2**.
   Prove your result using a table like the one above.
   You may find working with an example number a help.

It can be a bit cumbersome working with a 'number'.
Working with a letter standing for the starting number is easier.

B6 Find which of these sets of instructions fit the expressions below.

(a)
- Choose any number
- Multiply it by two
- Add five
- Multiply by five
- Subtract twenty-five
- Divide by ten

(b)
- Choose any number
- Add the number one larger than your original number
- Add eleven
- Divide by two
- Subtract the original number

(c)
- Choose any number
- Double it
- Add nine
- Add the original number
- Divide by three
- Subtract three

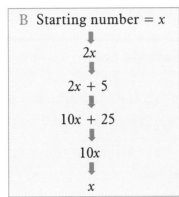

A Starting number = a
⬇
$2a$
⬇
$2a + 9$
⬇
$3a + 9$
⬇
$a + 3$
⬇
a

B Starting number = x
⬇
$2x$
⬇
$2x + 5$
⬇
$10x + 25$
⬇
$10x$
⬇
x

C Starting number = b
⬇
$b + b + 1 = 2b + 1$
⬇
$2b + 12$
⬇
$b + 6$
⬇
6

B7 Put these sets of expressions into instructions, like the problems above. Start off with 'Choose any number ...'

(a)
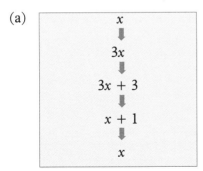
x
⬇
$3x$
⬇
$3x + 3$
⬇
$x + 1$
⬇
x

(b)
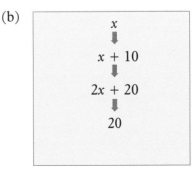
x
⬇
$x + 10$
⬇
$2x + 20$
⬇
20

B8 Try to make up some 'Choose any number' problems.
You might find it easier to start from the algebraic expressions.
Try your problems out on some other people.

B9 Which of these are incorrect?
How could you convince someone that they were wrong?

(a) $3(a + b + c) = 3a + b + c$

(b) $(2a + 2b) \div 2 = a + b$

(c) $5x + 15y = 5(x + 3y)$

(d) $5(x + 2y) = 5x + 7y$

Challenge

Here is a similar 'Think of a number' puzzle.
But this time it involves the spots on dominoes.

Here are the instructions and algebraic expressions which fit them.

'Pick a domino without telling me what it is. Then …'

Instruction	Algebraic expression	
Count the number of spots on the left-hand side of the domino	a	Let this number be a.
Multiply this number by five	$5a$	
Add seven	$5a + 7$	
Multiply by two	$10a + 14$	
Add the number of spots on the right-hand side of the domino	$10a + 14 + b$	Let the number of spots on the right-hand side of the domino be b.
Subtract fourteen	$10a + b$	If the answer is 32, which domino was chosen?

Work through the instructions and algebra with your partner.
How can you work out which domino was chosen?

Try the mind reading trick out on some other people.

C Expressions with dice

For a dice game the score is worked out using the expression $2r + g$ where r is the number showing on the red dice and g the number on the green dice. So four on the red dice and two on the green dice would give a score of $2(4) + 2 = 10$.

C1 Write down the scores when the dice show these numbers.

(a) Two on the red and three on the green

(b) Five on the green and three on the red

(c) Zero on the red and two on the green

(d) Three on both dice

C2 In another game the expression for the score is $2(r + g)$.

(a) What would be the score if there was nine on the red and one on the green dice?

(b) Joni wants to play this game but with the first person whose score is a prime number being the winner. What values on the dice would give a win?

C3 Make up some expressions for scores for yourselves.
Work out some winning conditions for these scores.
Try out the games for yourselves. Make sure the games are fair.
You may need to alter some of the expressions or winning conditions.

C4 (a) Find an expression for each of these scores.

(i)

Number on red dice	Number on green dice	Score
1	3	12
7	3	30
4	4	24
2	3	15

(ii)

Number on red dice	Number on green dice	Score
0	4	12
9	7	30
3	7	24
6	3	15

(b) Make up and try out some puzzles like these for yourselves.
 • One person decides on the expression without telling anyone.
 • The other chooses a number each for the red and green dice.
 • The first person gives the value of the expression with these numbers.
 • Repeat the last step until the second person can guess the expression.

D Expressions and perimeters

The perimeter of a shape is the distance
round its outside.

An expression for the perimeter of this square
is $a + a + a + a$ but we **simplify** this to $4a$.

A square of side a cm has a perimeter of $4a$ cm.

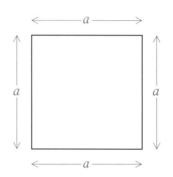

For the rest of this chapter all lengths are in centimetres, so the 'cm'
will be missed out.

D1 Here are some shapes made from four squares each of side a.

(a) Write down and then simplify an expression for the
perimeter of each of these shapes.

The first one has already been done for you.

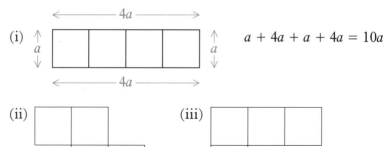

(i) $a + 4a + a + 4a = 10a$

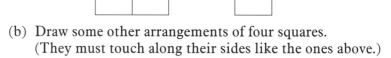

(ii)   (iii)

(b) Draw some other arrangements of four squares.
(They must touch along their sides like the ones above.)

Write down expressions for their perimeters.
Which arrangement has (i) the smallest and (ii) the largest
perimeter?

D2 Investigate the perimeters of
shapes formed when four
regular pentagons are joined
along their sides.
Each pentagon has side of length b.

An expression
for the perimeter
is $14b$.

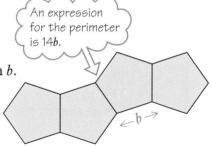

D3 Write down expressions for the lengths marked with ?.
The first one has been done for you.

(a)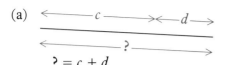

? = c + d

(b)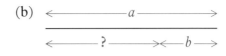

(c)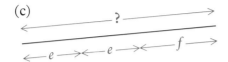

(d)

(e)

(f)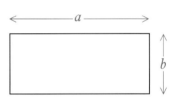

D4 This rectangle has dimensions a by b.
An expression for its perimeter is
$a + b + a + b$.
This can be simplified to
$2a + 2b$,
which could be written as
$2(a + b)$.

(a) Write down and simplify, as far as you can, expressions for
the perimeters of these shapes which are made from two
a by b rectangles.

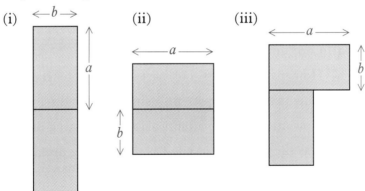

(i)   (ii)   (iii)

(b) Investigate the perimeter expressions for some other shapes
made from three a by b rectangles.

(c) Look back at your expressions.
What happens when $a = b$?

D5 Play the game 'Expression Solitaire' on worksheet B+ 7.

Review questions

1 Tables, charts and networks

1.1 This map shows some towns in Kent. Distances between the towns are shown on the road connecting them. These distances are in miles.

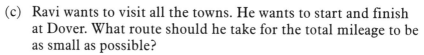

(a) Draw a mileage chart for these five towns.

(b) Draw a link table showing which towns are directly linked.

(c) Ravi wants to visit all the towns. He wants to start and finish at Dover. What route should he take for the total mileage to be as small as possible?

1.2 A drugs company has compared one of its new drugs with the existing drug. The number of people cured was found for each treatment. The results of this trial are shown in this two-way table.

	Existing drug	New drug	Total
Cured	600	450	
Not cured	200	150	
Total			

(a) Copy and complete the table.

(b) How many patients took part in the whole trial?

(c) How many of the patients using the new drug were cured?

(d) How many of the patients using the existing drug were cured?

(e) Was the new drug as good as the existing drug? Use some calculations to back up your answer.

1.3 Draw networks which have:

(a) Four vertices, two of them order two, one order three and the other order one

(b) Five vertices, all of order two

2 Pencil and paper 1   Do not use a calculator.

2.1 A jumbo jet can hold 445 passengers each weighing about 68 kg.

    (a) How much do all the passengers weigh in a full jumbo jet?

    (b) A tonne is 1000 kg. How many tonnes do the passengers weigh?

2.2 Investigate what happens when you multiply 37 by 3,   37 by 6,
37 by 9,   37 by 12,   and so on.

2.3 Here is a table showing the number of doctors and dentists for
every million people in the UK, Turkey and Mozambique. It also
shows the population in millions for each country.

Country	Population in millions	Number of doctors for each million	Number of dentists for each million
UK	57	1615	306
Turkey	52	741	164
Mozambique	15	21	6

Use the table to answer these questions.

    (a) How many doctors are there in Mozambique?

    (b) How many dentists are there in Turkey?

    (c) How many doctors are there in the UK?

    (d) Explain, in a sentence or two, what these figures tell you.

2.4 There are 170 more people in the world every minute.
How many is that in an hour?

2.5 The Ancient Egyptians used to weigh metals in debens.
A deben is 91 g. A gold statue weighs 254 debens.
What is this in grams? How many kilograms is this?

2.6 Oxfam recommend that a village well or pump should give
45 litres of water per person per day. How much water
will be needed to give enough for a village of 125 people?

2.7 There are 57 bricks in each row of a wall. The wall is 26 rows high.
How many bricks are there in a wall?

2.8 A jumbo jet uses 19 litres of fuel for each mile it flies.
How much fuel will it use flying from London to New York,
a distance of 5200 miles?

2.9 A Saturn V rocket develops as much power on lift-off as all the cars in Britain. There are 19 million cars in Britain. Each of these produces an average of 68 horse power. (An average horse works with a power of 1 horse power.)

If the Saturn V were powered by horses, how many would be needed?

3 Polygons

3.1 Draw an irregular pentagon. On your diagram mark and label the interior and exterior angles.

3.2 Is it possible to draw a polygon whose exterior angles are all larger than 90°? If it is, sketch it.

3.3 How would you convince someone that for any corner of any polygon the sum of the interior and exterior angles is 180°?

3.4 A regular polygon's exterior angles are all 10°. How many sides does the polygon have?

3.5 Find the value of these angles marked with letters. Try to give reasons for each step in your working.

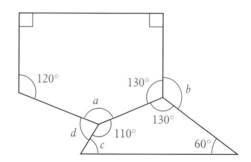

4 Polygons and symmetry

4.1 Write down the order of rotation symmetry and the number of lines of symmetry of each of these shapes.

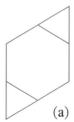

(a)

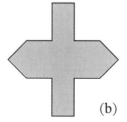

(b)

(c)

4.2 Draw an 8-sided polygon with 1 line of symmetry and 6 interior angles which are right-angles.

4.3 Write down what you know about the rotational and line symmetry of these polygons.

(a) Square   (b) Equilateral triangle

(c) Isosceles triangle (d) Regular pentagon

4.4 On a 4 × 4 grid investigate the symmetries of some of the patterns made by shading in four pairs of squares. For example:

4.5 Investigate the rotation symmetries of shapes formed by joining dots on a 5 × 5 spotty grid. Find shapes which have:

(a) Rotation symmetry and line symmetry

(b) Rotation symmetry but no line symmetry

Here are some examples.

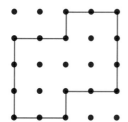 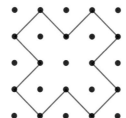 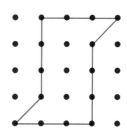

5 Significant figures

5.1 Round these numbers correct to 1 significant figure.

(a) 647   (b) 0·5327   (c) 6090   (d) 6·09

(e) 390   (f) 99·99   (g) 9·099

5.2 Round these calculator displays to 3 significant figures.

(a) 67·5432   (b) 0·006341   (c) 3·142

5.3 Work out the rough answers to these in your head by rounding to 1 s.f.

(a) 39 × 1·94   (b) 121·9 × 3·01   (c) 54·53 ÷ 11·01

(d) 997 × 6·3   (e) 9·7 ÷ 4·67   (f) 22 ÷ 5·09

5.4 Mark has to multiply together two 2-digit numbers.
He decides to estimate an answer by rounding each of the numbers
to 1 s.f. before multiplying them:

The estimated answer by rounding 59 × 11 to 1 s.f. is 60 × 10 = 600.
The exact answer is 649.

Investigate the size of the difference between exact and estimated
answers when multiplying two 2-digit numbers.

6 It's getting better all the time

6.1 Solve this problem.

'I think of a number, multiply by eight and subtract twenty-eight.
The answer is eight. What number did I first think of?'

6.2 I think of a number, square it and add the original number.
The answer is 90. What number was I first thinking of?

6.3 Find solutions, correct to 1 decimal place, for these equations.

(a) $x^2 + x = 3$ (b) $x^3 = 100$ (c) $x^2 + 2x = 16$

6.4 The formula $A = 3d^2$ gives the approximate surface area A (in
square metres) of a sphere whose diameter is d metres.

Use trial and improvement to find, to the nearest metre, the
diameter of a sphere whose surface area is 1000 m^2.

6.5 In the 1930s airships made journeys over the North Pole.
Crews found how high they were above the ice by timing
how long it took bottles of red ink to fall to the ground.
It was very easy to see the red ink on the snow!

Fall time in seconds was a square root of (the height in metres
divided by five).
Use trial and improvement to find how high an airship is for
a fall time of 5 seconds.

7 Transforming shapes

7.1 What effect does a clockwise rotation of 360° about the origin have on the point (2, 3)?

7.2 Here are some points and their images after reflection in the mirror line.

(a) Copy and complete the table showing the coordinates of the points and their images.

Object	Image
A(2, 3)	A′(3, 2)
B(1, 3)	
C	
D	

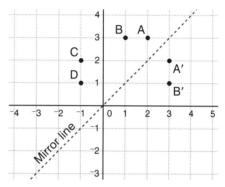

(b) Can you find a connection between each point and its image? Test your rule for some extra points – you will need to draw a grid of your own.

7.3 Andy says that reflecting the shape ABCD in this mirror line gives exactly the same image as if the shape was rotated through 90° clockwise about the point X. Is he right? Investigate for yourself.

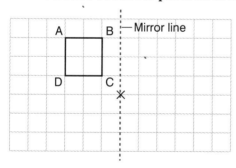

7.4 Here is a triangle ABC and its image A′B′C′ after a transformation. Copy the object and image on to squared paper. Try to find the transformation which changes ABC into A′B′C′.

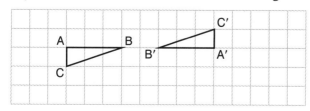

8 Pencil and paper 2 Do not use a calculator.

8.1 There are 16 ounces in a pound. One of the heaviest pearls ever found weighed 224 ounces. How many pounds is this?

8.2 What number multiplied by 23 gives 161?

8.3 Seventeen friends shared a prize of £544.
How much did each person receive?

8.4 A rectangle has an area of 598 cm².
Its larger sides are both 26 cm long.
How long are each of the shorter sides?

8.5 Before decimal currency was introduced in Britain there were 12 pennies in a shilling.
How many shillings were 156 pennies?

8.6 How many weeks are there in 105 days?

9 3-D symmetries

9.1 These models are all made from multilink cubes.
Make each model.

Ignoring connectors and holes, write down:

(i) the number of planes of symmetry of each model

(ii) the order of rotation symmetry about each of the axes shown

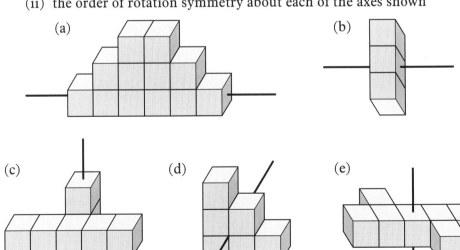

(a)   (b)   (c)   (d)   (e)

9.2 Which of these shapes have (i) an axis of rotation symmetry
or (ii) a plane of reflection symmetry? If you think the shape has
one or more planes of symmetry say how many.

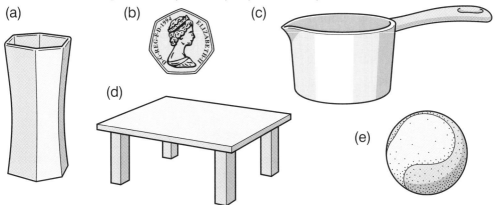

(a)　　(b)　　(c)

(d)

(e)

10 Negative numbers

10.1 Here are the highest and lowest temperatures for a town in Sweden.

	October	November	December	January
Highest	20°C	15°C	5°C	⁻1°C
Lowest	4°C	⁻3°C	⁻16°C	⁻20°C

In which month was the difference between the highest and
lowest temperatures (a) the greatest and (b) the least?

10.2 What is the sum of all the numbers from ⁻100 to 100 inclusive?
Explain how you got your answer.

10.3 Copy and complete this multiplication grid.
Draw in any 'lines of symmetry' you can see in the completed grid.

×	⁻10	⁻5	0	5	10
⁻10					
⁻5					
0					
5					
10					

10.4 The formula for converting temperatures in °F to °C is $C = \dfrac{5(F - 32)}{9}$,

where F is the Fahrenheit temperature and C represents the Celsius temperature.
Use the formula to convert these temperatures into °C.

(a) 32°F   (b) 0°F   (c) ⁻40°F

10.5 Read each sentence carefully. Decide if it is true or false. Give an example to support your choice.

(a) The sum of two negative numbers is always negative.

(b) The product of a positive and a negative number is positive.

(c) The square of a number can sometimes be negative.

(d) The product of two negative numbers is a positive number.

(e) Adding two numbers always gives a number larger than the two starting numbers.

11 Quadrilaterals

11.1 Write down the name or names of quadrilaterals which have:

(a) diagonals cutting at right-angles and one line of symmetry

(b) one line of symmetry and two pairs of equal sides

(c) one pair of parallel sides

(d) diagonals equal in length and bisecting but not crossing at right-angles

(e) all four sides and angles equal

(f) opposite angles and sides equal

11.2 Draw any parallelogram. On each side draw a square.

Find the centres of each of the four squares.

Join these four points up. What shape do you get?

What happens for other types of quadrilateral?

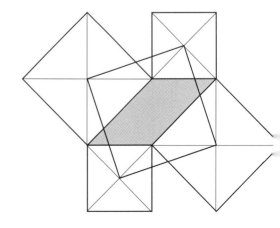

11.3 Investigate the possibility of having a quadrilateral that has these internal angles:

(a) three acute angles

(b) four acute angles

(c) a reflex angle and an obtuse angle

(d) two right-angles

Make a note of anything interesting you find.

11.4 Both methods A and B have been used by the Ancient Egyptians and Indians to find a rough estimate of the area of a quadrilateral.

A Find the product of the lengths of the diagonals.
Divide this by two.

B Find the mean length of opposite sides.
Multiply these two lengths.

Investigate how accurate each method is, by drawing quadrilaterals on squared paper. Does it depend on the type of quadrilateral?

12 Revisiting equations

12.1 Solve each of these equations and check them.

(a) $8x - 63 = 41$ (b) $13a - 48 = 43$ (c) $82 = 5a - 23$

(d) $14n - 99 = 5n$ (e) $37x = 18x + 361$ (f) $10a - 48 = 8a + 19$

(g) $11x + 4 + 13x + 6 = 22x + 26$ (h) $15x - 0 = 7 + 12x$

12.2 What value of b will give $9b - 27$ the same value as $6b + 81$?

12.3 Write down three expressions which have a value of $1 + x$.

12.4 Write down an equation for this puzzle and then solve it.

I think of a number (x), multiply it by 7 and subtract 28.
The result is 5 times the number I first thought of.

12.5 The pressure under water increases with depth.

The formula $p = \dfrac{d}{33} + 1$ gives the pressure p in atmospheres at a depth d measured in feet.

(a) What, to the nearest atmosphere, is the pressure 1000 feet under water?

(b) The world record depth for scuba diving was 437 feet in 1994. What is the pressure at this depth to the nearest atmosphere?

13 Expressions with letters

13.1 Write down three expressions whose values are:

(a) 1   (b) $a + b$ (c) $2x$ (d) $^-5$

13.2 CDs cost £y each. How much will ten CDs cost?

13.3 A coach holds 52 passengers.
How many passengers will a of these coaches hold?

13.4 In a certain triangle the three angles are such that the largest angle
is three times the smallest angle, and the other angle is twice the
smallest angle.
If the smallest angle is x degrees, write down an expression
involving x for the sum of the angles.
What is special about this triangle?

13.5 Make copies of this seven-dot grid on triangular spotty paper.

There are two different distances between dots. These are a and b.

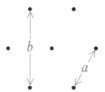

Investigate how many different quadrilaterals you can draw
by joining dots.
For each one, write down an expression for its perimeter.
Are quadrilaterals with the same perimeter congruent to each other?

13.6 Write down an expression for the output from each of these number
machines when x is input.

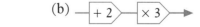

(a) $\times 3$ $+ 2$ (b) $+ 2$ $\times 3$

13.7 Simplify these algebraic expressions.

(a) $x + x + x$ (b) $2x - y + 10x + y$ (c) $3(x + y)$